SpringerWienNewYork

中国人民银
the cu
貨幣的未
伍 圆
JS96269764
THAT
EMA

STEFAN
SONVILLA-WEISS

SYNTHESIS AND NULLIFICATION

WORKS 1991–2011

SpringerWienNewYork

Professor Stefan Sonvilla-Weiss
Aalto University Helsinki / School of Arts, Design and Architecture

Supported by Aalto Arts

Printed in Germany

SpringerWienNewYork is part of
Springer Science+Business Media
springer.at

Cover illustration: Stefan Sonvilla-Weiss
Graphic design and layout: Stefan Sonvilla-Weiss
Copy editing: Cindy Kohtala
Printing: Strauss GmbH, D-69509 Mörlenbach

Printed on acid-free and chlorine-free bleached paper
SPIN: 80112721

With 91 figures

Library of Congress Control Number: 2011942342

ISBN 978-3-7091-1028-7 SpringerWienNewYork

For Barbara, Felicitas, Silvius

INTRODUCTION

During the making of this book I have learned that a retrospective of this kind is an exercise in learning to distinguish between the essential and the peripheral and to defy the gap. This endeavor attempts bundle all my passion and skills into designing and producing this piece of work, which should represent my theoretical and practical contention with visual culture over a period of twenty years.

I started this project in 2010 shortly after completion of the volume Mashup Cultures. It's tempting to apply to this book some of the core principles of mashups not least in terms of an additive or accumulative logic, in that mashups combine and collect material and immaterial goods and aggregate them into either manifested form or open-ended re-combinatory and interactive information sources on the web (cf. Sonvilla-Weiss 2010). Both this book and the corresponding website sonvilla-weiss.org seem to be a perfect match to counterbalance the static material and the dynamic immaterial world.

From its inception this project mainly revolved around the idea of showing concentrated and distilled artwork, design and essays along an invisible trajectory of recurring thematic areas and questions that allows the reader to make her own Ariadne's thread. One of the foremost challenges was to curate, represent and contextualize past and present theoretical and practical work so as to find the most accurate and stringent form of textual and visual approximation.

As this selection process can take time, many of the short stories as part of a bigger narrative went astray more than once. Over time I gradually immersed myself into the book design, which was joyful and much resembles the process of creating an art piece. Soon I realized that trying to review twenty years of work requires a) good documentation; b) an image archive of print quality; c) a catalog of search and classification criteria; d) stamina; e) rational thinking and hallucinatory immediacy; and f) a generous dollop of humor.

What helped me to narrow down the project scope was the decision to drastically reduce the display of artwork in order to avoid any resemblance to a catalog raisonné. Rather, my intention was to juxtapose the multitude of artistic research paths that were opened up to me by learning to understand how to use digital tools in different areas of applications in the early 1990s.

In retrospect an intense engagement with digital media gradually altered the way I looked at the mode of artistic practices, production, reception and perception beyond institutional spaces and discourse. This shift away from traditional artistic studio practice towards interactive and networked working practices marked a turning point in my professional career. One of the best "witnesses" to document these changes is my studio in Vienna, which over a period of 25 years "played the role" of a painting studio, multimedia studio, graphic design office, student flat, repository and a refurbished city apartment. This place is the context for digging into the archives of memorable anecdotes, one of which is worth telling. Having had completed one year of hard work on the tallest cardboard object I ever produced (see p. 199) the art piece was ready for exhibition. The movers came and tried to move the wrapped-up piece through the door frame. Soon it became clear that the 5 cm difference had to be sawn away from the horizontal part of the wooden door frame. Roland Barthes' "life is to live traces" still reverberates in my head.

The structure of this book follows a logic that helped me to organize and classify the multitude of forms and media. It starts with installations, presenting a selection of exhibited work between 1991-1997. Here I refer to artwork that has only partially been documented in previous catalogs. It has been a compelling experience to describe my own work from today's vantage point, borrowing and reconstructing the appropriate vocabulary from past deep experiences while reconfirming my presupposition that practice-based experiences are deeply engrained in our body's memory.

In the chapter on multimedia and photography I capture, amongst other things, my early encounters with computer-aided large scale imagery (CALSI®), a technique I experimented with in the mid-1990s. The unique characteristics of this image production – a combination of low res digital image and acrylic ink jet production – allowed me to discover new spatial and perceptual qualities as the image formats and contents stretched into hitherto unknown techno-aesthetic territories. The foundation on basic programming skills and digital animation that was laid during my MA studies in the early 1980s, while under different premises, was resumed and applied in interactive CD-Rom design and digital motion graphics along with the release of faster Apple computers and Macromedia Director multimedia authoring tools. In retrospect I noticed that during the mid-1990s quite similar working styles and production modes emerged amidst a burgeoning software culture (a term borrowed from Lev Manovich) that paved the way for artist coops who crossed over the canonical boundaries of low and high tech, popular and high culture, brands and subvertising, institutional and open spaces. One such collective is tomato (tomato.co.uk), a group of artists, designers, musicians and writers with whom I shared an affinity for cross-platforms and multimedia projects.

Running along the chronological order of my work the chapter texts and knowledge visualizations represent a selection of hitherto unpublished work that arose from my diary notes and sketches and the ongoing audiovisual blog entries called *daily reflections*. In addition the text on Open Source and Education that originates from late 1999 was translated from German into English. The idea behind the work in progress of the daily reflections blog entries, www.sonvilla-weiss.org, is to develop an audiovisual diary that reflects and represents my current thinking about how to better understand the complexity of mediated realities by means of sketches, videos, concept visualizations, design studies, animations and photography.

Later I decided to elaborate some of the intuitively emerged visual representations further into writing. To this end, I reassembled scattered text fragments with the aid of concept maps and rawly sketched synopses from the sketchbooks. A few of the short essays that resulted from this mixed media approach that evolved between 2010-2011 were selected for this book.

Over the years the fluid coexistence of analog and digital tools and modes of communication and creative production allowed me to extend my repertoire: my cognitive and emotional encounter with questions and phenomena circling around visual and media cultures. Some of the ideas and more or less elaborated representations and concepts that emerged from this contention are now put forward.

It would be my greatest reward to see that you, the reader of this book, take up what has been left incomplete and develop it further with your imaginative power.

Helsinki, 2012

THE

OF

NOESIS

WHICH

IS

OCESS

NING IS

THAT

S MEANT

DEMA

1
The process of meaning,
2009.
Color print,
60 x 42 cm

2
O and …,
2008.
Sketch from the
visual diaries
2003 – 2011

1

texts knowledge visualizations

THE CURRENCY OF THE FUTURE

Is gold, *bitcoin*, or *yuan* the currency of the future?

I suspect, rather I guess, that the currency of the future won't be money, the symbolic medium of exchange as we know it today, but instead another form of value-based, symbolic medium of exchange in which the definition of "value" will probably entail the most significant revision.

Virtual money reigns the world. Financial transactions across the globe are detached from labor and production of goods. Moneymaking is based on speculations of various kinds quite similar to gambling in which both rational calculation and fortuity is involved.

No one really understands the power unleashed by dehumanized, algorithm-based, computer-generated decisions made in a fraction of a millisecond that have become the driving force behind complete deregulation. Supranational hedge funds and financial tycoons speculate on collapsing currencies and national economies; private investors try to make strides on short-dated Greek government bonds with insurance against on the backseat, making money when the state goes bankrupt. The ones bringing down a state either by making them take a haircut or declaring insolvency are acting as the profiteers in all circumstances and possible scenarios. Either way, profit has always been generated at the material and financial expense of the majority of workforces. Now people are realizing that wage labor is keeping them in a condition of mere survival, while the wealth produced by his or her work goes to the corporate employer who controls its employees and to the shareholders who control the corporation.

Automatization, rationalization, and systematization that emerged from cybernetics and pervasive computation in almost all production processes accelerated productivity but caused in parallel disproportional benefits for management, workers, stakeholders and employers. Neoliberal policy abetted the payment of unjustified, high executive wages, marking out a previously seen, unfettered and uncontrolled dimension of greed, whose immensity cut off all previous relationships of wages to profit; in other words the relationship between labor productivity, average real wages and manager salaries became as speculative as the margins in the stock market.

Executive bonuses have become less the result of bought labor power to sell products than progressive investment policies based on highly risky and speculative derivatives. The more workers they dismiss the higher merits human resource managers earn from their companies. Or, the less or cheaper labor power an employer buys on maintained or increased productivity, the more profit he/she makes.

In times when companies felt responsible for their employees during and beyond professional careers, a bond of mutual trust arose from a worker's identification and affiliation with the products and the company's achievements.

Nowadays, the global economy forces international companies to erect and abandon their production plants at

3
Untitled,
2011.
Color print,
91 x 43.5 cm

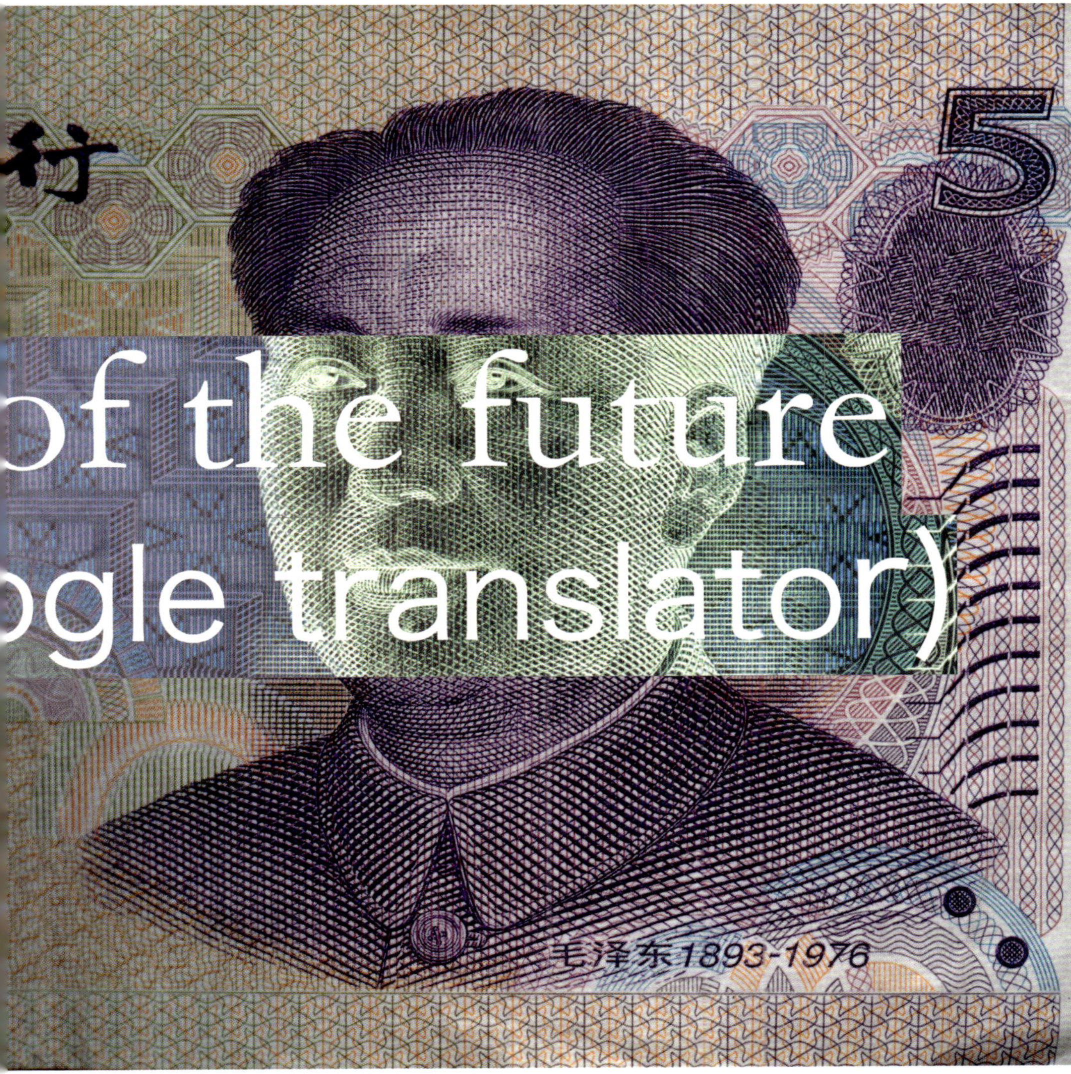
of the future
ogle translator)
毛泽东1893-1976

increasingly shorter intervals with the intention to always assure the cheapest labor and state or regional subsidies for providing new jobs. Once companies have fulfilled their contractual obligations to maintain production at the local site for a fixed period of time, they move forward to the next cheaper production site, leaving behind a wake of social devastation. These practices have been largely criticized by politicians who initially voted for neoliberal market practices and are now desperately trying to close the lid on Pandora's Box.

But this is not to bemoan the current situation but instead a calling to search for alternatives routes and initiatives that are already in place. While the Euro is under threat from predatory markets, at the same time the impact of a network society and economy are becoming more apparent as we enter the second decade of the twenty-first century. Apart from the justifiable anger manifest in street protests, such as the Occupy movement, there have been other responses to the crisis reminiscent of practices of sharing, collaborating, lending and bartering.

This goes hand in hand with the revivification in civil society activism, community organization and political grassroots movements seeking to renew and rethink our social bonds and affiliations. Peer-to-peer and social networks, creative commons, open source, and 'the crowd' are all proclaimed as new paradigms of possibility at which the disputes around public and private ownership of knowledge and culture have thrown the commons to the forefront of public debate.

Sharing is now a public virtue in the search for new open-access and open-source modes of sharing knowledge. Initiatives where cooperation and sharing are the basis for new economic models form alternatives to the market primarily in terms of resources and sustainability. Equally visible for decades now in the artworld are collectives built on a sustainable principle of production, where process, experience, authorship, responsibility and success are shared.

Money as we know it has an embedded architecture that leads to scarcity, centralization, concentration, secrecy, and proprietarization. This conventional monetary system is not appropriate to dealing with today's global systemic challenges: harmonizing local and global needs, creating ecological sustainability, enabling the information economy, leveraging the open source paradigm, etc.

The open money project, openmoney.org, pursues the goal to shift from centralized authoritative models to distributed ones that allow better sustainability, distribution, transparency, and regulation mechanisms. This kind of meta-currency system would enable a multitude of new types of money that puts currency creation directly in the hands of communities. Thus wealth-acknowledgment systems, tradable, measurable, and acknowledgeable, evolve in a feedback spiral with social cohesion and trust.

Key to understanding the concept of micro-currencies is a new form of wealth acknowledgment that provides the basic building blocks for communities to create new types of wealth acknowledgment systems themselves.

For example, communities can use open money systems

for local exchange trading systems, time banks, barter networks, carbon-emission trading programs, baby-sitting coops, business loyalty programs, and many more.

However, in view of the depleted natural resources on our planet Earth, the creation of sustainable wealth through alternative monetary systems of any kind won't suffice to face the challenges ahead. A possible alternative would be a rights and value-based economy that is in tune with our ecosystem. It is therefore essential that the health of the new economy is measured by the degree to which all human beings and the whole of nature prosper – and humanity must be seen as an integral part of nature.

The well-being of people and nature are our real inherited wealth that must be passed on to future generations. Elina Oström, Nobel Prize winner in 2009, is considered one of the leading scholars in the study of common pool resources (CPR), the way humans interact with ecosystems to maintain long-term sustainable resource yields.

Such a global commons-based economy would be linked to real value, human, and earth rights (p2pfoundation.net), consisting of:

1. *those aspects of nature and society that all people require access to in order to survive*
2. *a set of principles that would allow these to be stewarded by and held in trusteeship for the benefit of all*
3. *a set of appropriate values and norms.*

This will require that the global community:

1. *change the concept of ownership of nature to*

stewardship and trusteeship of the global commons
2. *modify the jurisdiction of the global commons*
3. *price its (ab)use*
4. *generate funds for the new rights and values-based global economy*
5. *create a currency based on the value of the global commons*
6. *shift our economic indicators and basic values and norms*
7. *shift from win/lose and win/win to all-win values and norms*
8. *look at the legal aspects of a rights and values based economy and*
9. *move forward without procrastination.*

Considering the money system and individual purchasing power as a social commons, there is a way to both stabilize and democratize money. Alternatively, the world community could create a form of monetary reference that is not dependent on the economic or political decisions of a single state or the money nationalism of currency-issuing states. Global commons representatives could collaborate to produce an international currency, backed by a new kind of reserve asset, to provide a stable and usable exchange credit for business trade and other social transactions. This new system would generate a broad measure of common wealth and well-being that is not based on productivity, profit or interest, but on the perpetual vitality and continuous adaptation of local resources to support a good quality of life for all human beings (cf. Ulatowska 2010).
(Helsinki, 2010)

CARTESIAN AND/OR CYBERSPACE

In the present discourse cyberspace entails manifold interpretations and concepts depending on the scientific field, application and usage in professional, private, creative and artistic contexts.

In William Gibson's 1984 novel Neuromancer, the original source of the term, cyberspace refers to a navigable, digital space of networked computers accessible from computer consoles, a visual, colorful, electronic Cartesian datascape known as *The Matrix* where companies and individuals interact with, and trade in, information. At present cyberspace does not consist of one homogeneous space; it is a myriad of rapidly expanding cyberspaces, each providing a different form of digital interaction and communication.

4
Search-cube, The Visual Search Engine, 2011.

The often-cited phrase 'lost in cyberspace' strikes me as an almost daily experience whenever the computer is turned on and connected to the internet. When browsing, searching and scanning information on the web I sometimes end up 'somewhere' unintentionally, unpurposefully and this situation often leaves me frustrated and scattered. Where did I start and where did I end up? The browser search history tells me the truth quite drastically: more than 200 different search queries this morning.

But what exactly happened when one hyperlink superseded the previous one, following a sudden impulse to click me away to the next page?

It must be a combination of discovery, curiosity, playfulness, disappointment, rational and irrational decision-making about whether the next click keeps a promise of newness, which is in fact a self-deception insofar as our limited perceptual capacities cannot keep pace with the invariant power of machine-generated stimuli. The result is either cognitive overload or a dissonance generated by the contrast of wishful imagination with factual reality.

In the physical world the steersman uses a navigation system on which the course and secure arrival at the final destination is reliant, whereas the cybernaut, the user who uses the internet, is confronted with a theoretically infinite number of options to navigate through rhizome-like dataspace. What is potentially an open-ended journey on the web conflicts with our corporeal limitations in time and space. From an anthropological standpoint, we have learned that a co-evolving part of humankind is the ability to create unbounded, parallel imaginative spaces of transformation, places that are not as they appear to be but as they are imagined or declared to be. It's tempting to speculate about the numerous thoughts, ideas, concepts and plans that remained in the imaginative dream world and those which have been manifested in the form world of time and space.

5
Lions, bear,
ca. 30,000 B.C.
Chauvet cave
paintings

What do we really know about the world of ideas and imagination that grew in people's minds preceding the world of physical objects? How many non-traceable creations of ancient cultures were there, hidden secrets of high cultures, representing the exploration and understanding of the spiritual and physical world?

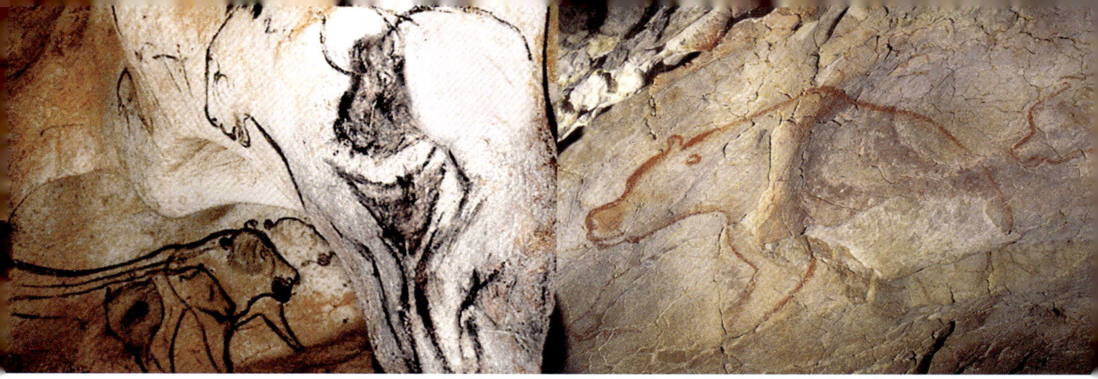

Only recently was I completely struck by one of Werner Herzog's last documentaries *Cave of Forgotten Dreams*, a 3D-movie about the Chauvet caves of Southern France, capturing the oldest known pictorial creations of humankind. The radiocarbon dates from these samples suggest that the periods of creation date back 35,000 years.

Besides the unique and extraordinary 3D-experience of co-exploring with the camera team the fascinating labyrinth full of magic wall paintings, which are usually not accessible for the public, the spectator becomes immersed in an archaic world of naturalistic depiction of animals and Chimaera. What is already mind-blowing in flat image reproductions becomes even more exciting as a 3D-viewing experience where you can see how the striking, naturalistic compositions of single or moving herds of deer are applied without distortion on curved and uneven rocky topography. This suggests that the maker of these wonderful drawings not only had the imaginative power to construct these mental images, but also the skills and tools available to depict them in manifested form. The powerful shoulders of bison, for instance, are often painted over a bulge in the rock that makes the muscles of the animal seem to swell realistically and gives the work a dimension that would have been impossible on a flat surface. They must have examined the wall closely first so as to find the places where the shape of the wall suggested animals or parts of animals before they began to paint. This meant that, at least some of the time, the cave artists had painted the animals suggested by the wall rather than imposing their own ideas onto the surface (cf. Curtis 2006).

From a morphological standpoint the drawings resemble Picasso's bull drawings, but in fact they are unprecedented in the virtuosity of the few significant strokes that depict these animals as expressive living, running, fighting creatures. It must have been a state of altered consciousness reached through trance techniques which enabled these Paleolithic cave painters more than 300,000 years ago to unite with nature in a state of magical mystical interplay in such a way that the depictions were experienced not as representations but as hallucinations provoked by sensory deprivation in the creative process. Quite similar to Lascaux, the Chauvet paintings will never be fully explicable for posterity, but they impressively show us that prehistoric cultures were already capable of making representational depictions, which no other culture could achieve in more than 30,000 years until Minoan culture came into existence.

A few thoughts struck me while I acknowledge there are quite a few speculations around how these culture phenomena would make sense within our rational scale of acceptable explanations. Arguably, the creation of such complex wall paintings and drawings is a combination of altered states of consciousness and mind exploration on the one hand and the process of rational and systematic planning on the other hand.

> *Prehistoric images are maps that enable their addressees to orient themselves in their environment. Their producers have stepped back from their own environment and into their own subjectivity. From this vantage point, they have been able to achieve a panoramic view of their environment. They have preserved this fleeting view in a memory and encrypted it in a manner that enables others to decipher it. Prehistoric images are subjective world pictures that are stored in memories. Once there, they are codified intersubjectively. Then they can be retrieved from memory. Thus, the designing subject is himself embedded in an intersubjective tradition: to a large extent, his code is preset. These images originate from a magical consciousness, and they produce magical behavior in their addressees. The consciousness is magical, because the environment, where things affect one another in reciprocal relations, is experienced as scenic: the eye hovers across the surface of the image and produces relations that may be reversed. The behavior of the addressees is magical, because the images are not experienced as a function of the environment, but rather the environment as a function of the images. There is a consciousness for which time circulates in space, to order space. And there is a behavior that works to obey the structures of time and space seen in the image. (Ströhl, 2002, 126 ff.)*

Cybernetic thinking links Flusser in a characteristic way to Ludwig Wittgenstein's philosophy in Tractatus Logico-philosophicus: "1.1 The world is the totality of facts, not

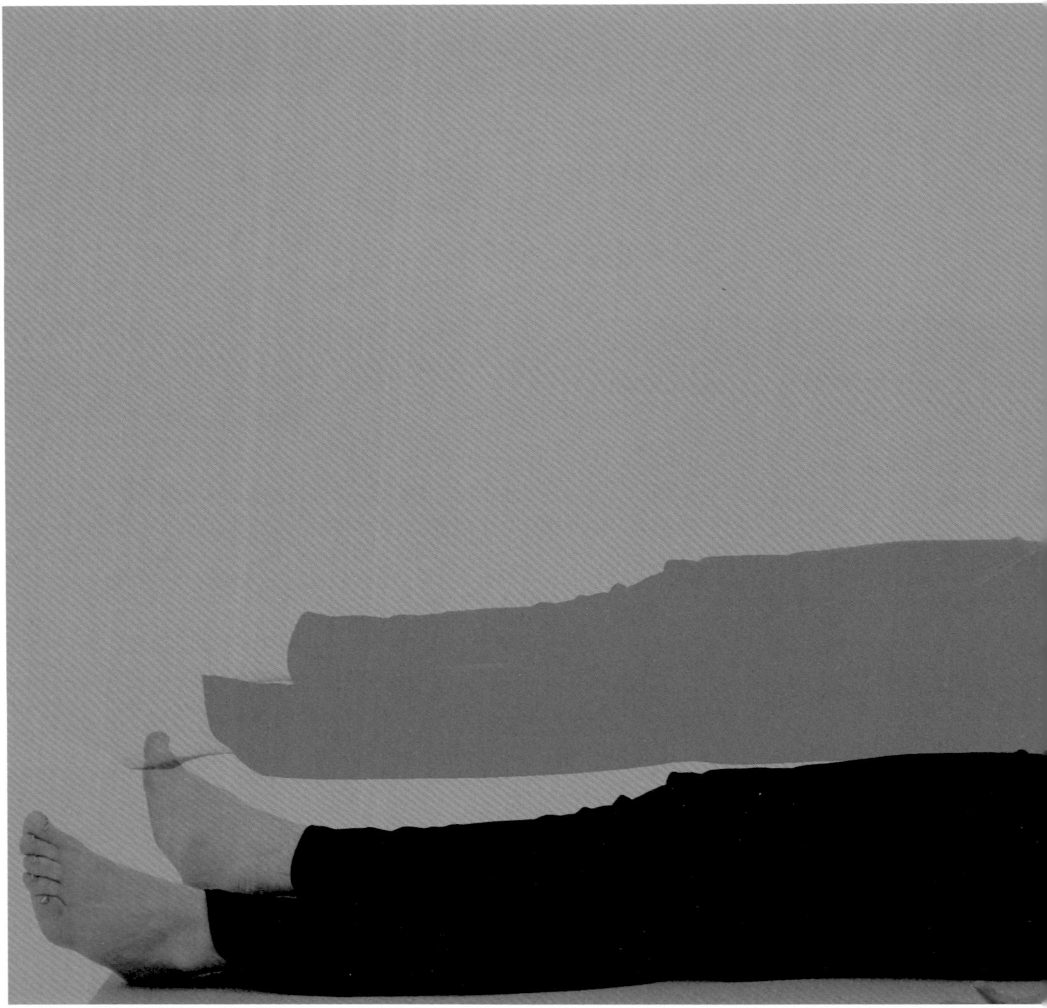

6
Out-of-body,
2011.
Still from the
animation

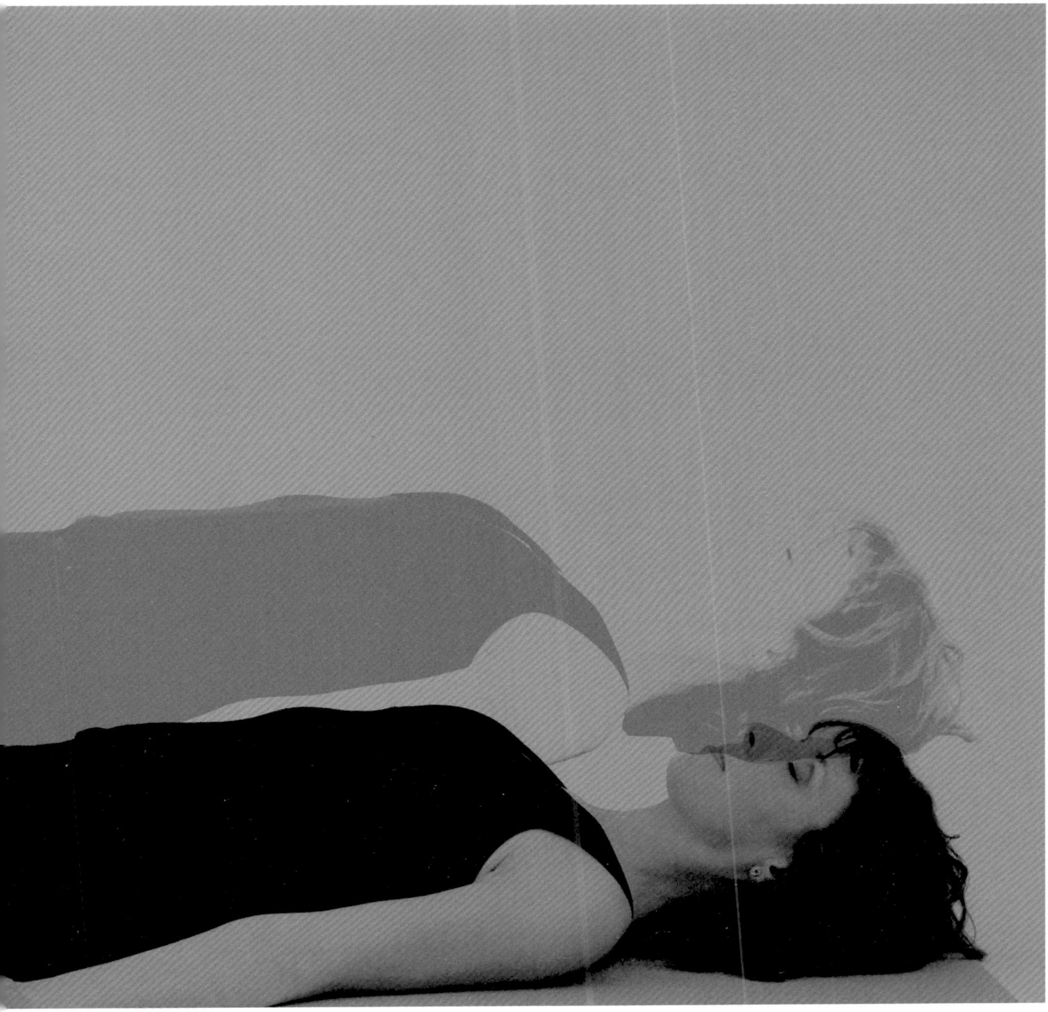

of things... 2 What is the case—a fact—is the existence of states of affairs... 2.01 A state of affairs (a state of things) is a combination of objects (things)." Relations, not things, are real; dialogues, not the men themselves, are relevant; the Self is a node in an entire network of connections.

7
Brain-Computer-Interface (BCI), 2010. Technische Universität Berlin

It is the entanglement of the virtual possible, the imaginative space, the spaces of communication and transfer and the manifested form in time and space that constitutes the basis of being and acting in the world. Thus real space can only be represented visually as virtual, but at the same time we always encounter a virtual space in a real space.

In combining real space and cyberspace interactions novel forms of synthetic space experiences could emerge, for example the creation of avatars in virtual worlds in combination with intelligent agents that execute a specific task on your mobile phone. The Euclidian model of space as a three-dimensional model of the real is only a simulation and thus follows the same principles of any other kind of representation, whereas in contrast cyberspace must be thought systemic, i.e. the various modes of human-machine interactions coevally reshape our radius of action in the social, private and public domain.

Ubiquitous access enables immediate action. We search for information on the web, bookmark and share it with others and thereby involuntarily give away private information to the service provider, or surveillance; scan and browse the web for never-ending bargains; create a blog to share our passions, hobbies and interests; jump into Second Life for the ultimate virtual encounter; build a microcredit

community for socially deprived people; organize a flash mob ...it's an almost endless list of possible scenarios, which views information as constructed and reconstructed by individual interacting in networked environments.

Early cyberspace concepts (Vinge, Gibson) perpetuated the Cartesian body-mind dichotomy, entailing a mechanistic worldview that has long since been superseded by the assumption that the brain exists in a body that lives in a world.

Hence consciousness must necessarily be thought of as embodied, whether it is necessarily embedded (or situated) in a social, cultural and historical context (cf. Haugeland

1998). One of the misconceptions of the term cyberspace is rooted in the metaphorical use of purely virtual existence, that is, communication on the internet does not take place in physical locations, but "in cyberspace." In a small side note, Gibson's statement in the documentary *No Maps for These Territories* (2000) is quite revealing: "All I knew about the word 'cyberspace' when I coined it was that it seemed like an effective buzzword ... evocative and essentially meaningless".

Cyberspace clearly denotes the site of computer mediated communication. Thus it must be understood synthetically, as an interconnected network of users, computers and servers. In this configuration real and virtual encounters take place at the same time. Thereby the "real" refers to the effects wheres the virtual denotes the intangible bit-level space, or data space. The impact of seamless switching between online and offline communication creates new forms of remediation between the "real" and the "virtual". By virtue of our dichotomous relationship with the natural world, the question is how these newly emerging synthetic spaces could turn collective intelligence into an upheaval of global consciousness.

(Helsinki, 2009)

8 *Cybernetic drawings,* 2003. Detail from the sketchbook

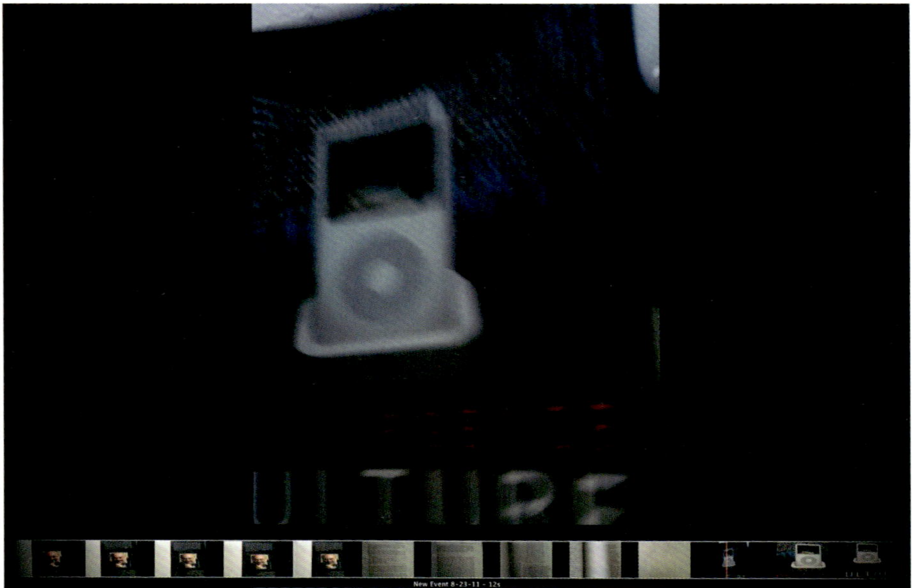
New Event 8-23-11 - 12s

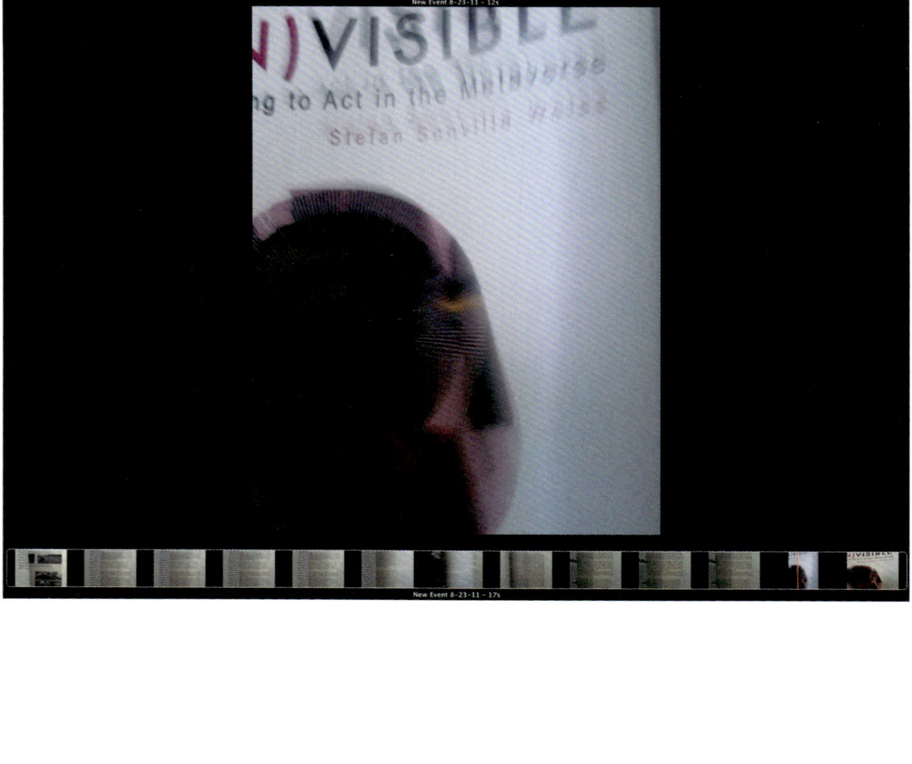
New Event 8-23-11 - 17s

SCANNING HENRY JENKINS AND STEFAN SONVILLA-WEISS

Almost randomly I took Henry Jenkin's book *Media Convergence* and my book *(IN)VISIBLE* from the shelf, opened them one after the other, and flipped through the pages at an excessive and increasing rate while filming these sessions with the recording device in my right hand. This playful encounter proposes a tangle of interesting questions about reading behaviors, our ability to scan, browse, read deeply and think attentively.

9
Stills from the recorded flip-book exercises, 2010

One morning I reshuffled and sorted out some books that had piled up on my office desk. I had been pondering over the causes preventing me from immersive reading experiences for some time. Was it the book content which often did not exactly meet my expectations, lack of time, or false expectations about newness and surprise? It happened frequently that after scanning a few pages books were laid aside and were never revisited again. Many of them, collected in boxes and on bookshelves, become empty shells, dust catchers made of letters, papers, the factual and the fictional. I always had a good eidetic memory which guided me quickly to the right location of the book, chapters, images and passages I was looking for.

However, admittedly, that was during a time when books were assiduously selected, carefully studied and placed on designated shelves. Over the years the amount of books multiplied to uncountable piles that gradually stretched out to the few remaining empty spots in the house.

Browsing a book can be fun and reminiscent of our first moving image experiences with flip-books during childhood. Browsing and scanning information at the same time is challenging especially when doing this in a constant flow, browsing through 300 pages within 5 seconds: in other words, 60 pages per second. It could be even faster or slower depending on my mood and sensomotoric skills in handling both the recording device in my left hand and the right scrolling thumb in a synchronized manner. Our sensual apparatus is conditioned to separately interpret a maximum of 16 images per second; above this threshold our brain interprets somewhere between 16 and 18 images per second as flowing movement.

The fascinating thing about flip-books is the simplicity of their making with maximum effect. In my specific setting, however, the curiosity was not so much in the phenomenon of the persistence of vision to create the illusion that continuous motion is being seen; rather I was intrigued by the parallel existence of human and machine perception.

This left dumb scrolling flip-book exercise, leading me to associations with real book scanning information archiving and retrieval, was then the initial trigger to ponder more deeply some of the epistemological and ontological consequences of machine reading, the digitization of all books existing on planet Earth in conjunction with the ever-increasing speed of information and knowledge production distributed and accessible over the net.

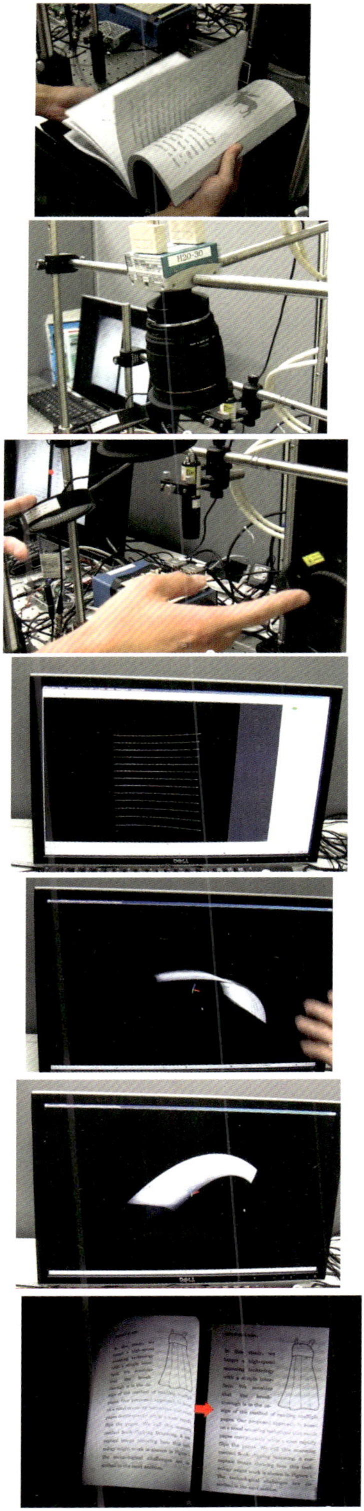

10
Book flipping scanning system, 2010. University of Tokyo

It seems that the rapidity of technological development is changing our reading behavior and the way we absorb and process information.

In his The Atlantic article *Is Google Making Us Stupid?* Nicholas Carr points to the demise of deep reading that has resulted from scanning and skimming information on the web. The style of reading promoted by the net privileges efficiency and immediacy over interpretation and reflection. Reading online is mere decoding of information "just in time" whereas our ability to make the rich mental connections that take shape when we read deeply and undistracted remains largely disengaged.

A good example that stands metaphorically and practically for "the clash" of human and machine recognition and perception are new camera systems that let you scan a book by rapidly flipping its pages in front of a high-speed camera. This method is called "book flip scanning." Essentially, in their research Takashi Nakashima and Yoshihiro Watanabe from Tokyo University embarked upon exactly the same prerequisites and equipment I used for my "scanning exercise" – a mobile phone and a flipping book. The key point in their research is how the system can decrease the user's workload when scanning document information on many pages.

Their Book Flipping Scanning is a new method of scanning large stacks of paper while the user performs a continuous page flipping action. The key technology behind it is a novel camera system that operates at 500 frames per second, with a resolution of 1280 by 1024 pixels. For each frame, the system alternates between two capture modes. First it shines regular light on the page and captures text and images. Then a laser device projects lines on the page and the camera captures that as well. The scanned pages are curved and distorted, but the researchers found a way to fix that. The laser pattern allows the system to obtain a page's three-dimensional deformation using active stereo methods.

The software they wrote builds a 3D model of the page and reconstructs it into a regular, flat shape. In the near future, the scientists hope to simplify and miniaturize the system to integrate it into portable devices like a smartphone.

Coming back to my playful flipping book exercise the intention was to create a performative and metaphorical action that spontaneously reflected the changing mode of reading into scanning and skimming of digitized information, which parallels the underlying dilemma of our limited perceptual and cognitive capacities (internalization) versus externalization of information and knowledge in databases.

However fascinating these newly emerging technologies may be – books and whole libraries will be scanned ever more rapidly in the near future – not only the access to these books is still limited, but also our capacity to overview, select, classify and contextualize "static" books and dynamic online information and knowledge resources. Absorbing information quickly and in bits and pieces has become a daily routine.

We've always skimmed newspapers more than we've read them, and we routinely run our eyes over books and magazines to get the gist of a piece of writing and decide whether it warrants more thorough reading. The ability to scan and browse is as important as the ability to read deeply and think attentively. Without doubt, reading a book, and taking the time to make inferences and engage imaginational processing, is more cognitively enriching than the short little bits you might get if you're into the 30-second digital mode.

Scientists speculate that reading on the internet may also affect the brain's hard wiring in a way that differs from book reading. Hence the question is whether it changes your brain in some beneficial way (Frey et al. 2010). Inevitably, under the premise that converging technologies, multitasking, audiovisual information gathering and processing pervades our daily professional and private communication routine, we need to search for technology-enhanced solutions that support our changing cognitive and emotional patterns of digital "reading" behaviors.

One such solution, although in a nascent state, is the *Text 2.0* research project (www.text20.net) from the German Research Center for Artificial Intelligence (DFKI in German). Their technology is capable of monitoring your eyes in order to define words if you gaze at them disoriented, eliminating non-essential information when you're skimming, helping you pick up exactly where you left off, swapping images based on what you're reading, surfacing relevant reference materials and more.

Think about the following scenario: written words are watching you reading them and making adjustments accordingly, and in parallel eye-tracking technology and processor-packed tablets will react, based on how you're looking at text – where you pause, how you stare, where you stop reading altogether. The act of reading will change what you are reading.

Taking more time to read certain words, phrases, or names could trigger the appearance of sound effects, footnotes, translations, biographies, definitions, or animations. If the user begins skimming the text, the tracker will begin fading out words it considers less important to the text. If the reader glances away, a bookmark automatically appears, pointing to where the user stopped reading.

The current version of "augmented reading" devices are still under development, but the fusion of different sensing modalities that include voice, finger ID, facial expression, biometrics, and gaze vector technology proposes an augmented intuitive and media-rich browsing, skimming and deep reading experience.

That's by no means a plea to abandon traditional book reading, which activates and cultivates our imaginative power like no other medium; still, keeping up with the accelerating speed of information and knowledge production and access requires augmentation of audio-visual and text-based information that enhances the user's current perception of reality. But unlike virtual reality that replaces the real world with a simulated one, augmented reality bridges and takes advantage of the real world and the simulated world.

What started as a playful book flipping exercise reminiscent of early childhood and continuing experimentation with moving images eventually led me to a much deeper investigation and exploration of epistemological, technical

and aesthetic questions of book reading in the near and the far future. On a more general note, playfulness and initial undirected and unpurposeful encounter with the things around us gives us the freedom to create something new. Hence I would like to conclude with the plea to preserve these powerful spaces of creative flow.
(Helsinki, 2010)

11
Repair, 2007.
Sketch book
drawing detail

REPAIR ≠ RECOVER ≠ RESET ≠ RESCUE ≠
SAVE ≠ PROTECT ≠ REVIVE ≠ RELEASE ≠
REFORM ≠ RECONNECT ≠ RELINQUISH
REMOVE ≠ SURRENDER ≠ EVOLVE ≠

NO ENTRANCE FOR
HUMAN BEINGS

NO ENTRANCE FOR HUMAN BEINGS – A SIMPLE SHORT FICTION

If I imagine a situation that sees me standing in front of a door where there is a sign mounted saying, "NO entrance for human beings", then I would certainly start wildly speculating about ALL POSSIBLE SCENARIOS behind the door.

Provided that the sign has been fabricated and designed in a human environment which from our understanding is the only species on earth capable of producing such a sign, the logical consequence is that the one who created the message must know what is behind the door.

12
No entrance for human beings, 2011. Draft for a wall design

Spinning this idea further I start wondering if what I see in front of my eyes is simply meant as a provocative statement that ought to make us think about an all-encompassing understanding of living creatures on Earth.

Secondly, the text containing this prescription not to enter the space behind the door is mounted on a door in a building which is institutional and access restricted by law. It is evident that the text "No entrance for human beings" has been created and designed by someone who works in the building or has been instructed and authorized by someone else to fabricate and mount the prohibitory shield on the door. In that case the person who commanded this action must have had the intention to put up this sign on that specific door.

No one has ever witnessed anyone disappearing behind the door. A camera on the ceiling and an automatically generated signal when the door opens have full control over the door and would register any attempt to break into it.

Up to now, nobody has ever figured out who gave the order to produce this sign and to mount it on the door. All employees in the building were forced on pain of penalty to declare their non-involvement in any kind of activity that might have produced the aforementioned result.

Who was the originator and why is the sign still in place?

13
Design of a
PGP word list,
2010.
Color print,
63 x 45 cm

14
Inside-Outside,
2011.
Infographics

The following story has been translated into human language. By chance it is in English, but it could be in any other existing living language on planet Earth. It is said that somewhere along the way there was a war between the government and privacy advocates on the use of effective

0	aardvark	adroitness	15	backfield	bifocals
1	absurd	adviser	16	backward	bodyguard
2	accrue	aftermath	17	banjo	bookseller
3	acme	aggregate	18	beaming	borderline
4	adrift	alkali	19	bedlamp	bottomless
5	adult	almighty	1A	beehive	Bradbury
6	afflict	amulet	1B	beeswax	bravado
7	ahead	amusement	1C	befriend	Brazilian
8	aimless	antenna	1D	Belfast	breakaway
9	Algol	applicant	1E	berserk	Burlington
A	allow	Apollo	1F	billiard	businessman
B	alone	armistice	20	bison	butterfat
C	ammo	article	21	blackjack	Camelot
D	ancient	asteroid	22	blockade	candidate
E	apple	Atlantic	23	blowtorch	cannonball
F	artist	atmosphere	24	bluebird	Capricorn
0	assume	autopsy	25	bombast	caravan
1	Athens	Babylon	26	bookshelf	caretaker
2	atlas	backwater	27	brackish	celebrate
3	Aztec	barbecue	28	breadline	cellulose
	baboon	belowground	29	breakup	certify

encryption. The government claimed full control over private encryption and decryption keys, considering the right of the general public to protect their own data as an impediment to government law enforcement.

One day, the public got hold of the secret cryptosystem and discovered – what has long been in the air – a parallel world of citizen existence, a gigantic collection of data, stored and classified in never before seen virtual quantum units. Up to now, none of the designated physicists, cryptographs or programmers were able to fully decode this data into a human readable form. The new government decided to label ongoing investigations top secret ending up in a complete information stoppage policy.

Rumor has it that a group of hackers got into the system and cracked sensitive data from industrial espionage, illegal financial transactions and private intimate issues.

15
Suspicion,
2011.
Infographics

Steve wants to send Olivia a secret email that he doesn't want to be stored in a national security database, nor to be shared with anyone else who shares the open accessible wifi network in their flat-sharing community.

Olivia learned about a public key cryptosystem that uses two different keys for encrypting and decrypting data. This public key cryptosystem is called PGP (Pretty Good Privacy). Both Steve and Olivia will have their own key pair consisting of a "secret key" (used with a secret password to decrypt all encrypted messages and files) and a "public key"

So Olivia for example uses her public key to encrypt a message to Steve, and he in return will use his secret key to decrypt the message. Both could also use their public key to encrypt their own files and use their secret key to decrypt them. In principle, the public key could be given out to anyone without compromising security.

In fact, an outsider could only encrypt a message, but without having the "secret key" there is no way to decrypt this information.

16
Public key,
2011.
Infographics

A CAPTCHA (Completely Automated Public Turing test to tell Computers and Humans Apart) is a program that can tell whether its user is a human or a computer. Most web users are familiar with them — colorful images with distorted text at the bottom of web registration forms. Many websites deploy CAPTCHA to prevent abuse from "bots", automated programs usually written to generate spam. Hence bots cannot navigate sites protected by CAPTCHAs, nor can any computer program read distorted text. However, as a human being I am capable of responding adequately to the challenges of reading and inserting CAPTCHA distorted letters and numbers.

Several software companies then came up with the idea to twist the imperfection of OCR (Optical Character Recognition) scanning of old books with crowd participation via CAPTCHA applications.

Numerous projects (not only Google) are digitizing vintage books, documents, maps and prints that were created before the digital age. This striking initiative aims at archiving human knowledge and to make information more accessible to the world.

The book pages are being photographically scanned and transferred into text, which is useful because scanning a book produces images that are difficult to store on small devices, expensive to download, and cannot be searched. The transfer from analog to editable, digital readable formats calls for human participation to improve the process. Words that cannot be correctly interpreted by computers are then used in CAPTCHAs for humans to decipher.

But what happens if a computer can't read such a CAPTCHA: how does the system know the correct answer to the puzzle?

17
CAPTCHA design, 2011.

18
Air seats 2012, 2011.
Concept design

Steve receives directly by email from the OCR automatization process each new word that cannot be interpreted correctly by OCR. Thereby he gets another word for which the answer is already known. He is then asked to read both words. Steve remembers that he shares with Olivia the private key to decrypt highly confidential messages. Steve passes on to Olivia the word for which the machine could not retreive the correct word (answer). Now Steve holds both the correct interpreted word by the machine and the unknown word. It is then assumed by the system that if the user solves the one for which the answer is known, likewise the answer will be correct for the new one.

Olivia holds now the word for which the machine could not find the appropriate answer. She deciphers the correct word, which Steve approves over their private key communication channel and they both agree.

Guess what happens if the system then gives the newly identified word (image) to a number of other people to determine whether the original answer was correct...?
(Helsinki 2011)

FROM SOFT CINEMA TO COLLABORATIVE MOVIEMAKING IN THE CLOUD

Why do we take, collect and share such enormous amounts of mediated worldviews? What are we going to do with this overwhelming bulk of digital representations? Is it a re-assurance of our own reality construction in the multiverse?

19
Social media distributed systems model, 2011.

In the pursuit of the apparatus, from Freud's "prosthesis god" to "the extension of men" (McLuhan) to wearable computers (Steve Mann), single user interaction has shifted into multiple user interaction on various platforms with either time-based (video sharing), image-based (photo sharing), text-based (blogs and wikis) or audio-based (podcasts) focus. The driving force behind this global move towards self-expression, authenticity and community building is rooted equally in human nature's inherent narcissism and the basic desire to belong to a specific group. Both extremes, idiosyncratic exposure and social networking, are phenomena that do not constitute media culture per se, but rather belong to a newly observed phenomenon in current Web 2.0 developments.

In my attempt towards a visual evidence-based analysis of some of the most prevalent global connectivity phenomena based on mobile imaging and ubiquitous data exchange, I will start with a short narrative that would also support in that specific context the idea of identity construction in interrelated spatial/temporal, socio-cultural and media-technical contexts.

The frozen glass tripartite in front of me is framed like a triptych containing live images. Some elements within the framed reality are static; a few of them are moving around vertically and horizontally on the imaginary screen. A plane wipes from right to left and vanishes in undefined time and space. Three-dimensional perception interferes with two-dimensional invisible traces, markers and ephemeral reflections on the glass canvas.

What if the fragile and transparent wall broke into a thousand pieces? ... The glass is just a weak membrane between reality and illusion, and I am sitting and waiting. How do I gain a grip on the essence of my thoughts that motivated me to reflect on certain phenomena at exactly that time, situation and space?

20
Still from the animation *Aesthetics of Uncertainty,* 2010.

I start sketching and recalling fragmentary visual mnemonics (memory aids) but I cannot exactly remember the spatial dimensions and details of the furnished environment inside the Schiphol airport building.

I am shooting images with my thinking eyes. Images are floating thoughts, unless I capture some of them in manifested form.

I search for thoughts, stimuli and sometimes reality.

The process of visually reconstructing mental images has just begun (cf. Sonvilla-Weiss 2008, 54). The search function on Flickr allows me to specify my search for a similar image that both matches the main tags such as "waiting", "airport", and "Schiphol", as well as a kind of visual resemblance to my original concept. Surprisingly the search results that match the keywords amount to 57 photos.

Instead of checking all thumbnails in search of the visual manifestation that comes closest to my imaginary mosaic, I type in the additional tag "gate" that scales down the image retrieval to seven photos tagged with "airport", "waiting", "schiphol" and "gate".

Finally I get a result that rather satisfactorily makes visible what I had in mind. Hence I become the eyewitness to and investigator of my own visual memory. The objective is to achieve a "likeness" of my pictorial record made up of various parts or blended memories bearing close similarities, characteristics and resemblances to my sketch. The global database has become our collective visual memory. It makes no difference if I take pictures on my own or let them be taken by anyone else on the globe.

Mobile imaging with a camera phone, driven by an autobiographical impulse and a yearning for authenticity by means of self-recording devices, is key to the enormous amount of digital image production and distribution on the web. In contrast to first-person forms of documentation based on narrative logic (photo albums, diaries, or scrapbooks), mobile imaging engages with accumulation and recombination as associated with a database logic. One of the consequences of this shift is that mobile imaging implicates its practitioners in assortative circuits of tracking. In this context digital shooting functions as an extension, an externalized memory of visual attractions, but it also revises the impetus self-reflexiveness. The apparent compulsion towards continuous imaging, a result of the device (potentially) always being in hand, drives a persistent and continuous awareness: an alerted attention towards potential shooting.

21
Screenshot from *Flickr* website containing the search queries "airport", "waiting", "schiphol", 2010.

The act of self-evidencing leads to never-before-seen image production, comprising an ever-expanding visual statistical archive. Taking photos by mobile phone engages the practitioners to comprehensively participate in the circulation of images and tracking functions.

Considering the exorbitant number of images produced, dispersion of accumulated photo streams are rather approached across series than in distinct personal episodes. (cf. Sonvilla-Weiss 2008, 56)

In my book Mashup Cultures (2011, 9) I explain how

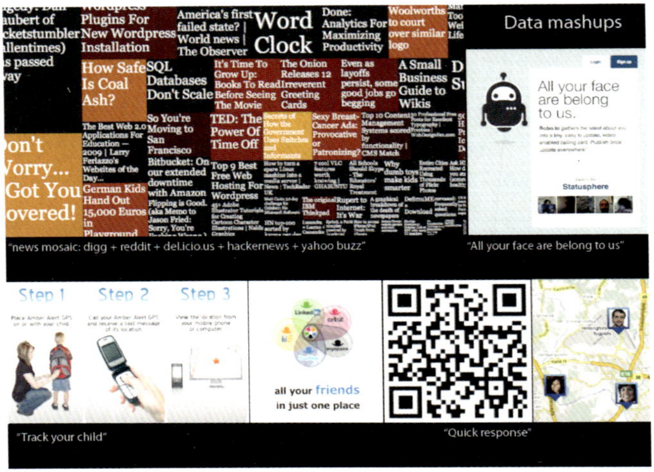

22
Data mashups, Infographics, 2010.

previous remix practices are significantly differentiated from today's mashup cultures, insofar as collage, montage, sampling or remix practices all use one or many materials, media either from other sources, art pieces (visual arts, film, music, video, literature etc.) or one's own artworks, through alteration, re-combination, manipulation, copying etc. to create a whole new piece. In doing so, the sources of origin may still be identifiable yet not perceived as the original version.

Mashups as I understand them put together different information, media, or objects without changing their original source of information, i.e. the original format remains the same and can be retraced as the original form and content, although recombined in different new designs and contexts. For example, in the ship or car industry standardized modules are assembled following a particular specific design platform, or, using the example of Google Map, different services are over-layered so as to provide parallel accessible services to the users. Remix and mashup practices in combination can be considered as a co-evolving, oscillating membrane of user-generated content (conversational media) and mass media.

In 1969 Peter Greenaway released one of his first short movies "Intervals". Adapting Vivaldi's notation system from The Four Seasons, Greenaway presents a series of images shot in Venice, purposefully avoiding any presence of water.

23
Still from Peter Greenaway's short movie *Intervals* (1969).

His sequence structure is exact and countable: one series of images is repeated three times while the soundtrack grows in levels of sophistication.

Intervals was the first Greenaway film to gain distribution and is made in the structuralist style, paralleling the films of Hollis Frampton with its repetitions of sequences, variations in editing rhythm and a soundtrack.

Greenaway's shorts are resistant to storytelling. Each film

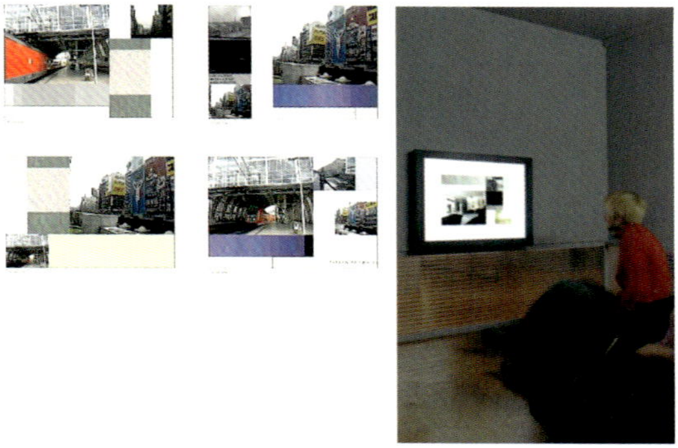

24
Soft Cinema, 2003. Installation commissioned and produced by ZKM

essential presents a list of items, similarly to a database that represents the world as a list of items.

Databases (re)define the narrative form so that it can be construed as a particular trajectory through a space of possibilities and meanings. Lev Manovich treats narrative and database as two conflicting representational impulses with the former emphasizing a cause and effect chain of events and the latter a list of disparate elements. This theoretical tension between narrative and database is manifested in Soft Cinema films as two competing interpretive systems through which the spectator can impose coherence onto the films.

Soft Cinema attempts – with varying degrees of success – to question the ways computers and software-based art can be used to represent contemporary "distributed subjectivity", a project that Manovich likens to the literary modernist projects of Proust and Joyce (cf. Manovich 2005).

With our "selves" continually scattered across corporate

databases and surveillance systems, Manovich looks to the networked computer as a more revealing metaphor for understanding contemporary identity than the linear, cinematic narrative.

Soft Cinema makes use of a mode of dynamic, real-time image assembly in which viewers offer no input beyond the initial selection of which piece to view. Once a project is launched, the Soft Cinema engine executes a series of choices, guided by carefully designed parameters and rules (algorithms), in order to deliver a narrative experience that varies each time it is played. The result is a kind of "ambient narrative" in which narrative meaning and aesthetic coherence must be discerned or constructed by the viewer. Experiments with this type of decentered authorship – from Marcel Duchamp's readymades to Andy Warhol's Factory – have characterized modern art since the early 20th century.

Christopher Nolan's film *Memento* from 2000 is often used to show the distinction between plot (narrative) and story. The main protagonist's loss of memory in this movie can be equated with an artistic means to alter the story itself or influence the response of the viewers when they tell the plot in a seemingly arbitrary order.

Memento's narrative structure is unusual in that we are not shown the story from beginning to end, but rather from end to beginning. In the first scene, this is literal because the startling opening shot/conclusion of Leonard shooting Teddy in the head is reversed, so that the bullet jumps back up into Leonard's gun.

However as the film progresses, the footage is shown

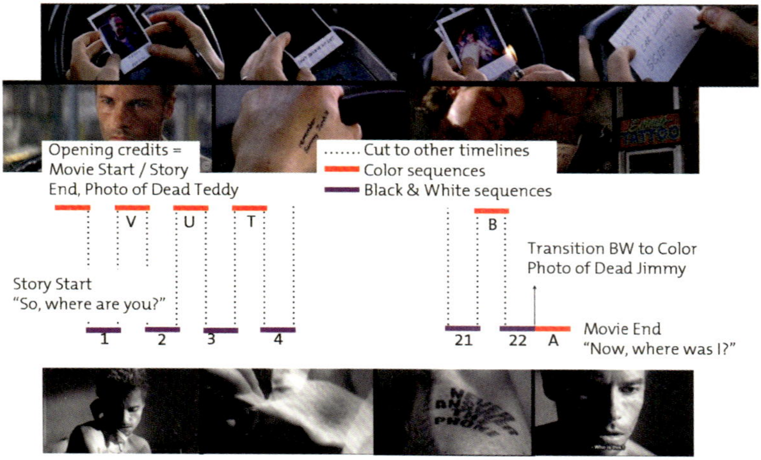

25
Plot structure of the film *Memento*

normally, but segmented and in reversed order. Nolan thus applies reverse chronology in his movie, a method of storytelling whereby the plot is revealed in reverse order.

In a story employing this technique, the first scene shown is actually the conclusion to the plot. Once that scene ends, the penultimate scene is shown, and so on, so that the final scene the viewer sees is the first chronologically.

Many stories employ flashback, showing prior events, but while the scene order of most conventional films is A-B-C-etc, a film in reverse chronology goes Z-Y-X-etc..

The film's events unfold in two separate, alternating narratives — one in color and the other in black-and-white. The black-and-white sections are told in chronological order, showing Leonard conversing with an anonymous phone caller in a motel room. Leonard's investigation is depicted in color sequences that are in reverse chronological order. As each sequence begins, the audience is unaware of the preceding events, just like Leonard, thereby giving the viewer a sense of his confusion. By the film's end when the two narratives converge we understand the investigation and the events that led up to Teddy's death.

Here the fabula (story) / plot (narrative) timeline is depicted as a numbering scheme from 1-22 for the black-and-white sequences and letters A-V for the color ones.

The plotting of the film as presented is: Opening Credits (shown "backward"), 1, V, 2, U, 3, T, 4, S, ..., 22/A, Credits.

The short clip we have seen showed a smooth transition from the black-and-white sequence 22 to color sequence A, which occurred during the development of a Polaroid photograph.

A combination of lifelogging, crowdsourcing, mobile imaging, digital storytelling, global connected databases and networking culture led to one of the most popular crowdsourced mobile imaging projects named "Life in a Day". The concept of the film is that producer Ridley Scott and Oscar-winning documentarian Kevin Macdonald requested footage shot anywhere around the globe (including under the sea and in the air) on a particular Saturday (the fitting date 24/7, as it is written in Britain).

The material, submitted by literally anyone via YouTube, could be of any length and shot with any kind of camera, whether digital or film. Macdonald then constructed a 90-minute feature compiled out of these submissions, most of which were cut down to mere snippets displaying

common, mundane everyday activities. The result is a montage depicting a day in the life of planet Earth. Technically it's the latest documentary classifiable as crowdsourced or user-generated cinema, yet the collaborative effort becomes distorted through the film director's single person vision.

In other words, it is not the content being concentrated but the economic value of content. MySpace, Facebook, and many other businesses have realized that they can provide free production and dissemination tools but maintain ownership over the resulting products. The long tail (Anderson 2004) of the niche strategy of certain businesses (e.g. Amazon) allow them to realize significant profit by selling small volumes of hard-to-find items to many customers, instead of only selling large volumes of a reduced number of popular items. It appears that the fundamental economic characteristic of Web 2.0 is the distribution of production into the hands of the many and the concentration of the economic rewards into the hands of the few.

YouTube has just launched an official gallery showing off some of the 80,000 submissions it received as part of its Life

26
Stills from the collaborative movie *Life in a Day*

in a Day project. The official gallery is viewable as a matrix or as a 3D sphere. You can sort through videos based on location, time of day, mood, the type of place where the video was shot and more.

Clearly this rudimentary mode of interaction stands in stark contrast to the potentiality of participative systems and the emancipatory use of media. One could also argue that the entire setting implies a conceptual lag which privileges algorithm-based narrative segments over story. In this case the fabula of story, the social fabric of story, loses its voice. Each single voice or each video posted on YouTube suggest that story shapes identity differently from narrative.

However, the online version of Life in a Day ignores the aspects of collaboration that is "working jointly with". Unlike interaction and participation, the term collaboration implies the production of something with a degree of equality between the participants. Collaboration between people is an inherently participative and interactive process that can be well observed in for example the open source cinema and wreckamovie collaborative online platforms.

All these initiatives are rooted in Richard Stallmanns GNU Manifesto from 1987, which in my opinion not only revolutionized software culture but, to a much greater extent, fundamentally altered our concepts of material and immaterial good in favor of liberating source code from any kind of ownership towards the concept of open source. That's why I feel it is important to reproduce some of Stallmann's key thoughts leading to the Free Software movement:

27 *Technical Difficulties,* Concept work, 2010.

> *You have the freedom to run the program, for any purpose.*
> *You have the freedom to modify it to suit your needs.*
> *You have the freedom to redistribute copies, either gratis or for a fee.*
> *You have the freedom to distribute modified versions of the program, so that the community can benefit from your improvements.*

Cloud computing drives the many social media sites that you access virtually every day. At the same time the more complex the hard- and software, which is essentially defined by its usability and modes of interaction, algorithms, metadata, formats, and protocols, the more difficult it is for the individual on both the micro and macro level to piece together these fragmented parts into a whole new picture in the very metaphorical and practical sense.

I therefore consider Defragmentation to be a key concept

in networking culture, trying to re-establish alienated modes of common understanding through aggregation, augmentation, reconfiguration and combination of information, quite similarly to what the hard disk does when physically organizing the contents of the disk to store the pieces of each file close together and contiguously.

From the standpoint of information sciences information is defined by its existence as a bit – in Bateson's formulation, "a difference that makes a difference." This is an important aspect insofar as it holds an immanent power relationship: that of control within a complex system of hierarchical order and manipulative control mechanisms. Control of information and communication equates with control of code, leading again to fundamental questions: "Who is the owner of the code, where is it stored, and what are the consequences of misuse?"

Code is the language of our time, as there is hardly any consumer article in our daily usage free of computer-supported, automated mass production chains. Our cultural production with all its pluralistic modes of expression and formats produces a parallel digital universe that is stored in and dispersed through a gigantic network of databases around the globe.

Richard Stallman was right with his call for "Free Software", as it engages with non-exclusionary and non-hierarchical forms of co-evolvement of intellectual goods manifested in code for the purpose of constant improvement in an open source environment. Many attempts have been made to translate open source principles into the broader cultural realm (cf. for example Lessig's *Free Culture*) yet under the wrong premises of mixing commodity value up with intellectual value, which does not necessarily generate surplus value but rather exchange value. The value of code, then, is not generated through multiplication of single copy software products but instead through exchange of different versions, modifications according to needs, specific needs a piece of software should fulfill. "You can buy a picture, but you cannot buy the image in it" might work as an analogy for liberating code from any kind of commodity boundaries.

In other words, code must circulate freely to build upon collective intelligence, something that has been convincingly demonstrated as a successful business model in almost all big ICT branches. Free software does not mean that everything is for free: it can for example lead to new business models and products in which code remains free and modifiable by the open source community.

Comparably, in Mashup Cultures the code that makes possible information and knowledge exchange must be maintained liberally as a public good. Important steps in this direction are APIs (Application Programming Interfaces) that allow web communities to create an open architecture for sharing content and data between communities and applications.

In this way, content that is created in one place can be dynamically posted and/or updated in multiple locations on the web; for example photos can be shared from sites like Flickr to social network sites like Facebook and MySpace.

The interconnectivity of software applications and their

users on the web appears from today's perspective a literacy with which most teenagers and prosumers are familiar. Yet the impact of such a remarkable media revolution as that of Web 2.0 on individuals and society at large can only be fully understood in a media-historical context: understanding what and how communication media has transformed within the complex interplay of perceived needs, competitive and political pressures, and social and technological innovations.

(Helsinki, 2009)

THE INTERNET

28
The Internet of Things, 2009.
Detail from
unfinished
media project

AD HOC COMMUNICATION

I began to be drawn in by ad hoc communication concepts after learning about aid initiatives in earthquake-devastated areas where small wireless networks were temporarily arranged to maintain at least some basic telecommunications. In view of the many sensitive zones on Earth that are either endangered by natural forces or human-made disasters, alternatives to company or state-owned and distributed communication services must be sought and solutions must be provided to keep up at the very least basic telecommunication channels. The term HASTILY FORMED NETWORK (HFN) was coined after Hurricane Katrina to describe impromptu networks that provide crisis communications, such as those formed in the aftermath of Haiti's earthquake.

29
Quick Response,
2010.
Mobile design study

Why I am taking up this example as an introduction to ad hoc communication and (future) networking has less to do with apocalyptic prophecies than with an interest in how vulnerable our communication technology is on the one hand and on the other hand how much infrastructure and resources from outside are required to rebuild broken communication networks.

Going back in history, I came across Victor Papanek's groundbreaking guide to ethical design theory *Design for the Real World*, which sheds light on industrial design through a user-centered design framework.

One of Papanek's best known user-centered projects is the

30
Victor Papanek, *Tin Can Radio,* 1962.

radio receiver 'Tin Can Radio' (Papanek 1984). This product was requested by the United States Army based on the assumptions that people in "third world" countries are illiterate and unaware of national agendas. The communication device the army had in mind would not require batteries or any form of external power input. Papanek came up with a solution comprising a used juice can, paraffin wax and a wick as its power source.

The rising heat was thereby converted into enough energy to power the receiver. This simple mechanism could easily be maintained with additional wax, paper, dried cow dung, or anything else that would burn.

Seeing the extremely low manufacturing cost of 9 cents per unit (by 1966 US standards), Papanek envisaged people would assemble these radios themselves to ensure independence from outside parties for the ongoing

31
XO laptop,
2005. Design
sketch

production of the product. Comparing this self-made approach from 1962, which at that time brought out a radical and innovative method in design thinking, with today's complex ICT devices and infrastructure, it appears almost impossible to apply similar self-empowering methods to current standards. Closest to this retro grassroots approach from the 1960s, which radically echoed Sullivan's apodictic statement "form follows function" from the late 19th/ beginning of the 20th century, comes newly blossoming "green", trashable, upcycling social (media) design projects.

Clearly Papanek's radio receiver is outmoded in technical terms, but the concept gains fresh momentum for a whole movement of sustainable and socially responsible designs for products and tools.

Perhaps Negroponte's OLPC initiative from which the 100 Dollar XO laptop emerged could be regarded as a similar socially engaging approach although under different conditions. Ad hoc or mesh networking is a key feature of these educational laptops. Its main characteristics are the use of a wireless backbone and the existence of multiple routes due to radio interconnectivity. XO's mesh network follows the new IEEE802.11s standard, which is still in a nascent state, but preliminary results show that the mesh network is functional up to 550 meters without an antenna. Ad hoc here in the very literal sense applies to the whole initiative of digital inclusion.

Almost 50 years after Papanek's low tech radio receiver, later smartphones, laptops, tablet computing and cellular infrastructure, data-intensive technologies are capable of aggregating and distributing different sources of information to the average person. Through this rapid access to information the individual becomes a source of information as well as a consumer. Crowdsourced data is now becoming a major source of information sharing for first responders.

For example, in the 2010 Haitian earthquake response, VoIP, video and applications like Skype, Ushahidi (crowdmap), Sahana, OpenStreetMaps, Facebook, Twitter, Google Maps, and many other social media and crowdsourced applications provided some of the communication and situational awareness for disaster responders (Nelson et al. 2011).

It is this multitude of communication channels, devices, protocols and operational use of mobile technology that co-creates adaptable and modifiable networks. While I am pondering existing areas of applications in the car industry it comes to mind how prone and error-sensitive our closest communication devices are.

> *No signal, no connection. I have tried again and again to get my mobile phone working. The battery should be almost full, or did I forget to charge it last night. The automatic Wi-Fi network finder function is activated. Usually a multitude of random networks pop up, but most of them are protected. 3G saves me again as it connects to me to the internet.*
> *I imagine a situation where there is no longer any digital communication network available in a post-digital age.*
> *I am closing my eyes, I am connecting with those people with whom I'd like to share something.*
> *No more annoying emails, spam, phishing and fishing. Emails gone, mailboxes, web tools, networks forever lost. No digital info, movies, sound or infoscapes, distracting or avoiding elements, effortless scrolling browsing navigating, everything occupying my thoughts. Suddenly I can see things in front of my eyes. I am the messenger and the message. Where is the next bus stop? On the road people are following the scattered signs; information is passed over to the people next to me.*
> *A man with a walkie-talkie desperately presses the button to get his message through while the child in close proximity repeatedly calls for his mom. Not far away is a collection point where people get first aid and information on their relatives …*

Provided that our global communication system is at least partly working, a flexible, ad-hoc communications network can create connectivity in remote, developing or disaster locations where communications is often unreliable or non-existent. It is an infrastructure-less, wireless network

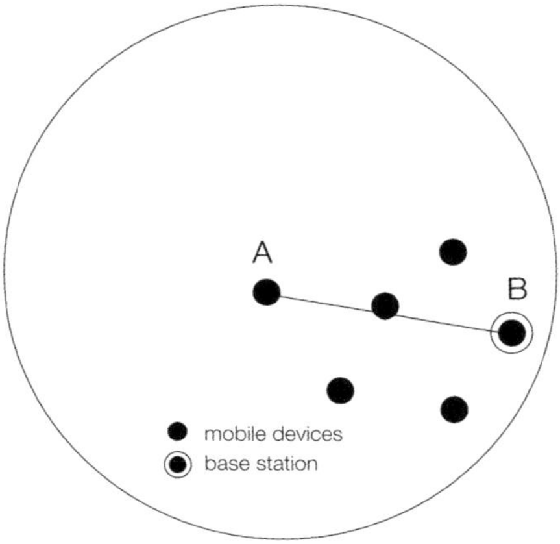
A
B
mobile devices
base station

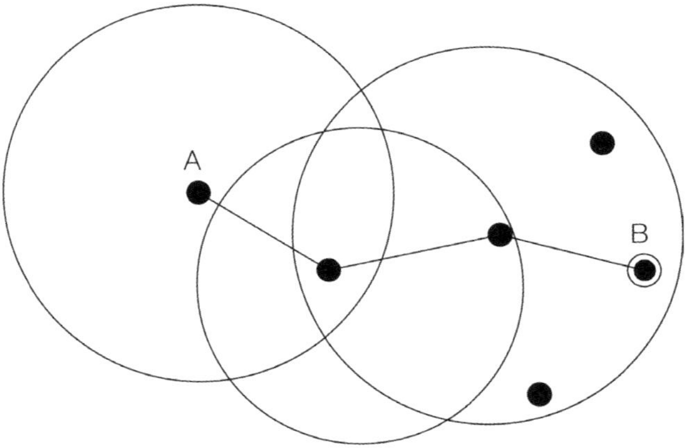
A
B

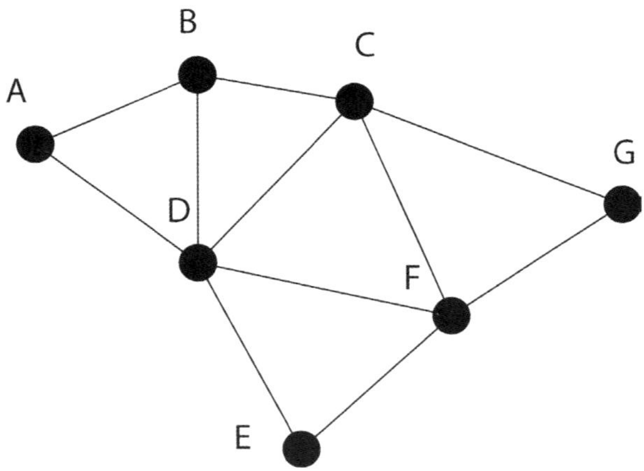
A
B
C
D
E
F
G

that can cover areas from a few hundred meters to a few kilometers in diameter and is formed out of consumer devices or nodes. Every node in the *LifeNet* network acts as a host and a router at the same time, making a centralized governing body unnecessary for operation. The network created by *LifeNet* can grow or decrease incrementally as users can connect or disconnect at will. Moreover, all devices across a *LifeNet* network can access the internet if one device has connectivity. *LifeNet* is open source software using the free Wi-Fi spectrum and commodity Wi-Fi protocol for link layer communication and is a self-configuring Linux kernel module.

32
Ad hoc networks,
2008.
From mobile to infrastructure-based networks

But how does an ad hoc network operate in a very broad technical terms?

For example, the top figure (left) depicts a situation in a traditional mobile communications network: Device A sends data directly to a base station B. This means that only the spectrum in circle A is loaded. A must continue to supply energy for transmission. Thereby the energy required depends at least on the square of the distance from A to B.

The middle figure depicts the same situation in which the different end-systems work as a mobile ad hoc network to support data transmission. Device A passes its data to the next end system, which is located close to the base station. At the same time each end system that receives the data examines in turn a subsequent operation, to which the data are transferred until the base station is reached.

Looking at the bottom figure, one can see that the applied load of the spectrum was reduced to a smaller area. In addition, the sum of the squares of the individual distances covered is smaller than the square of the distance from A to B. Therefore, the sum of the energy consumption of all individual transfers is smaller than the energy required for direct communication from A to B. Because of these properties it is to be expected that mobile ad hoc networks will be used in the future as an access network to infrastructure-based networks.

In other words, the direct way is not always the most energy efficient one. In the physical world car sharing and ride sharing is better environmentally and presumably more energy saving than any individual car drive. Ideally, in a city space where there is scarcity of parking spaces and lots, an automatically generated map on your mobile showing you the closest bus, metro, or car sharing station, while at the same time calculating time, consumption, life cycle assessment, possible traffic jams or construction areas, guides you to the most appropriate carrier. Urban dwellers are more and more refraining from adopting the car as a status symbol and replacing it with flexible and efficient mobility arrangements. Ad hoc communication management holds great potential for almost all our encounters with our natural and built environments.

33 *Material, immaterial value chain,* 2010. Concept design

This convincing example of shared information transfer is reminiscent of the concept of P2P and its expanding usage of relational dynamics in distributed networks, which is not just computer to computer but human to human. One of the proponents of commons-based peer production is Yochai Benkler who examines the ways in which information

connect share valuate exchange

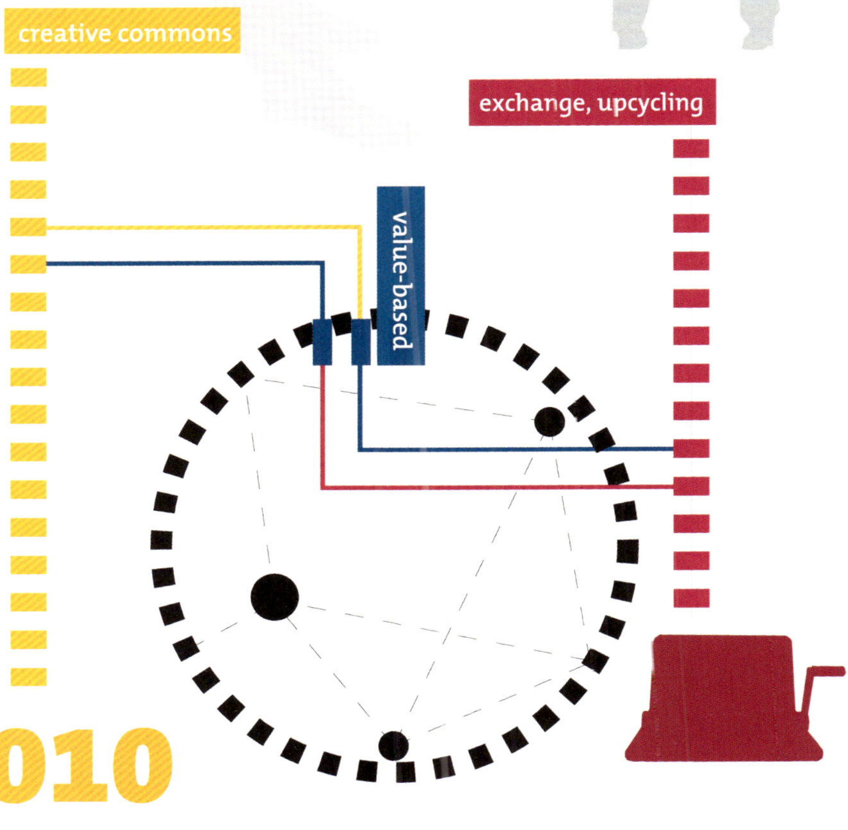

010

technology permits extensive forms of collaboration that have potentially transformative consequences for the economy and society.

But what are the benefits of enabling virtual communities to self-organize and introduce incentives for resource sharing and cooperation? Arguably, the principles of P2P are less understood by the majority of users, who still remain in consumer mode. Coevally, the conceptual design of file sharing communities encourages illegal downloads and thereby entails the irreversible negative effects on fair exchange of intellectual property on the web.

To this end, the whole P2P operational mode needs to be revisited and adjusted to ethical principles of trustable and reliable forms of material or non-material exchange. In the process of drafting a flexible, ad hoc sharing model I imagine an interface that enables visualization of transactions among individuals, flow and exchange of material and immaterial goods, accountability, reliability and trustworthiness, use and reuse of resources and information in order to build a sustainable network of reusable and recyclable products, and an open and transparent user account displaying modes and contents of transactions as well as peer group feedback. This could then lead to simple queries: "where is the next free car sharing opportunity in return for a collection of sources for energy efficient housing". Ad hoc communication translates here into intertwined modes of collaboration and sharing based on possible mutual benefit.

(Helsinki, 2011)

34
Public, 2009.
Concept design

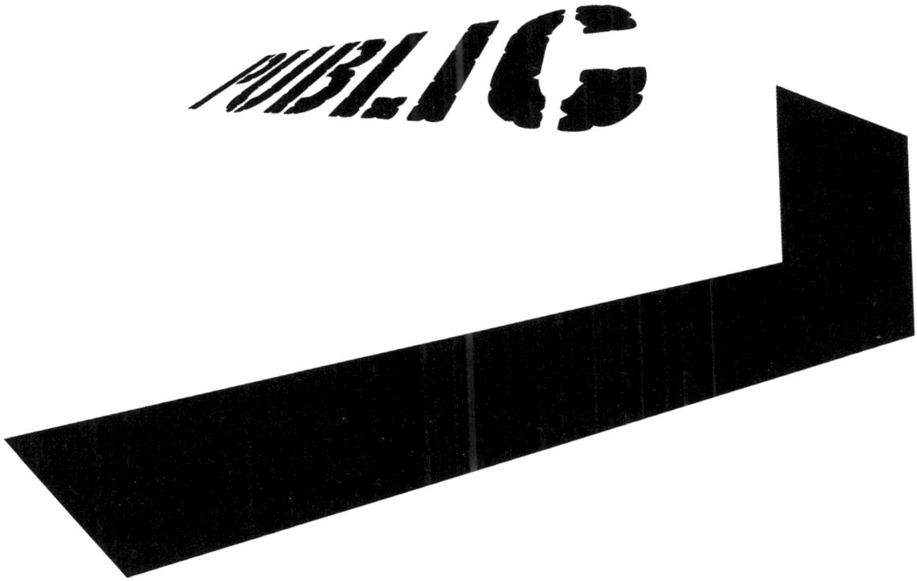
PUBLIC

HACKING ETHICS AND CIVIC ENGAGEMENT

Hacking is not limited to computers. "Cultural Hacking – the Art of Strategic Action" (2005) for example deals with subversive efforts to escape the branding machine of the media and corporate retailers. Thereby strategies of subversion and symbolic exchange in search of a revised Cultural Studies approach take up practices from Dadaist and Situationist movements.

35
Change is gonna happen, 2007. Public intervention

In my book *(IN)VISIBLE,* I argue that cultural allusions are reduced to stereotypical signifiers that provide the constitutive elements used by advertising to signify the impact of globalization caused by neo-liberal economic practices. The global presence of a particular corporation serves as apparent proof that corporate practices are beneficial to all peoples. The amplification of capital as it flows across the globe at an accelerating pace searching for higher rates of return makes use of advertising to legitimize its power as it transforms socio-cultural environments (Klein 1999). As a consequence, originally subversive works and ideas are themselves appropriated by mainstream media and are offered lucrative contracts in return for partaking in 'ironic' promotional campaigns.

Slavoj Zizek (1989) argues that the kind of distance opened up by cultural jamming provides the possibility for ideology to operate: "...by attacking and distancing oneself from the sign-systems of capital, the subject creates a fantasy of

transgression that 'covers up' his/her actual complicity with capitalism as an overarching system."

Without going too much into the details of hacking history, it is important to understand its origin and initial purposes; for example, a "hack" has always been a kind of shortcut or modification – a way to bypass or rework the standard operation of an object or system. The term originated at MIT in 1960 with model train enthusiasts who hacked their train sets in order to modify how they worked. These and other early computer hackers were devoted programming enthusiasts, experts primarily interested in modifying programs to optimize them, customize them for specific applications, or just for the fun of learning how things worked. In many cases, the shortcuts and modifications produced by these hackers were even more elegant than the professional programs they replaced or circumvented. During the 1970s public awareness of hacking became apparent when a different kind of hacker appeared: the *phreaks* or *phone hackers* that were part of emerging cultural jamming activities such as hactivism, marking out a completely new direction of subversive strategies and techniques against corporate culture.

It is thus important to shed light on the skills and attitudes of software hackers, and the traditions of the shared culture that originated the term "hacker" as Eric Raymond has put it so aptly in *Hacking, Open Source, and Free Software*.

Still striking today are his remarks on "Status in the Hacker Culture", which in retrospect make plausible the core principles of social networking. As Raymond concludes, hackerdom runs on reputation: whether your solutions are truly good is something that only your technical peers or superiors are normally equipped to judge. More specifically, hackerdom is a gift culture, by giving away your time, your creativity, and the results of your skills.

The *Pirate Manifesto* (Gupta 2009), an attempt at a fundamental rights-based platform for the Pirate Party movement in Sweden (http://www.piratpartiet.se) and Germany, puts forward key points on digital labor and its cultural, political and economic implications. I will pick up a few points from their core goals, which can be considered as first steps towards awareness-raising in the political establishment about the many issues of privacy, surveillance and infrastructure in a networked society. The following passages concentrate on questions regarding how we can find better solutions to ensure intellectual property and at the same time anchor, adept and modify copyright laws, individual and common rights, cultural heritage and privacy according to changing professions, modes of production, labor, and living, networked, parallel existing societies.

Core issues are the protection of citizens' rights, the will to free our culture, and the insight that patents and private monopolies are damaging to society. To better understand this, the film "RIP: a remix Manifesto 2.0" hosted by *Open Source Cinema* is highly recommended. Each of the movie's chapters, for example *Copyright vs Copyleft, The Past tries to control the future, Back in the People's Hands, The Revolution will be digitized*, links well to the arguments raised in by the Pirate Party claiming that copyrights were originally created to regulate the right of a creator to be recognized as the creator and have later been expanded to cover commercial copying of works, also limiting the natural rights of private citizens and non-profit organizations.

What the Pirate Party criticizes is that economic and technological developments have pushed copyright laws far out of balance, unjustly favouring a few large market players at the expense of consumers, creators and society at large. So, for example, millions of classic songs, movies and books are stored in the vaults of huge media corporations, not wanted enough by their focus groups to re-publish but potentially too profitable to release. However, cultural heritage must be accessible to all; a fundamental concern is that ideas, knowledge and information are by nature non-exclusive and their common value lies in their inherent ability to be shared and spread.

The services and support non-profit organizations like Creative Commons provide for scientific and academic communities is only a first step in probing legal sharing, use, repurposing, and remixing of cultural, educational, and scientific content that is available to the public for free. Change in commercial copyrights struggles with balancing conflicting commercial interests, and suggestions to reduce commercial copyright protection, i.e. the monopoly to create copies of a work for commercial purposes, to five years from the publication of the work is unlikely to be achieved in the near future.

36 *Pillow flashmob,* Berlin

In the spirit of Open Source, Free Software and General Public Licenses, the new political movement is an important voice for Generation "Web n+1", trying to respond to existing and new challenges digital life poses to individuals and society in finding new answers to safeguard citizens' rights: their right to privacy and basic human rights.

In this vein, civic engagement in public spaces as a tool, practice and technique needs to be rethought and reorganized with regard to synchronous forms of real and virtual communication by means of social media. *Flashmobs* are a good example of how quickly a large group of people can assemble in a public place, perform an action for a brief time, and then quickly disperse.

What sympathetically discerns *flashmobs* from *smartmobs*

is the fact that *flashmobs* do not necessarily have a purpose, although they may express an opinion or a statement. In other words, the definition of smartmobs emerged from smart mob technologies and their impact on communication and cooperation, in both a beneficial and destructive manner: for example used by some of its earliest adopters to support democracy and by others to coordinate terrorist attacks.

Flashmobs in contrast put the ephemeric event character into the foreground, which can be socially, culturally, politically, or artistically motivated using compound tools and methods for transmitting the instructions either by email, SMS, forums, discussion groups, or word of mouth.

From the *Flashmob Manifesto* we can learn how generation "Web n+1" develops performative and activist skills and competences to convey their messages in public spaces in playful appropriation and re-interpretation of historical *happenings*, which are a form of participatory new media art, emphasizing an interaction between the performer and the audience. In breaking the imaginary "wall" between "performer" and "spectator" *happenings* include everyone present in the making of the art and there are no set rules, only vague guidelines that the performers follow. What both *happenings* and *flashmobs* have in common are a) short durations; b) ad hoc arrangements; c) focus on mass consumption; d) mass spontaneous participation; e) novelty and creativity; f) freedom from form restraints; and g) location independence, to name only a few.

However, today's mainly politically motivated *flashmobs* bring into play a set of rules and guidelines considered prerequisite in order to communicate and operate effectively and distinctively within a determined time frame and event purpose, for example in the following way: a) a *flashmob* must remain discrete; b) the mobbers do not communicate with one another during the *flashmob*; c) the gatherings must happen at an exact time and the mob must not last more than 10 minutes; d) a single person can create a *flashmob*. Although the popularity of flash mobbing is short-lived and its style is deliberately ephemeral, its popularization is well documented by blogs and mainstream media primarily because of the use of mobile communication technologies.

In conclusion, the hacking ethos developed in the early

open source movement has irrevocably changed consumer mass media culture into a participatory media culture, which has established novel forms of user engagement and interaction with the public domain both on- and offline. In that *remediation* has turned into a signifier of fluid real and virtual world enactments, Generation "Web n+1" continuously explores the permeating boundaries of technology enhanced modes of production, reception and perception in interdependent socio-cultural and political contexts.
(Helsinki, 2009)

OPEN SOURCE AND EDUCATION

The idea of Open Source, which has led to a process of rethinking software development even in big corporations, is connected consistently with the notion of open sources of knowledge that offer knowledge, instead of source codes, in many different presentation modes. Linux and Free Software in schools increasingly compete with standardized operating systems and software products. This is due to growing awareness among teaching staff that the organizational processes of a mediatized teaching and learning culture must amount to something more than a "rush to catch up technologically"; they instead need to obtain a corrective by way of what is known as "soft key qualifications".

In this context, the model of Linux is not only considered as a "soft-technological" product, but is increasingly being discussed as an ideological "bundle". In the field of servers, Linux caught on worldwide with the Apache software; many schools see it as an opportunity to make their networks, strained by students, safer and more efficient after expensive standard solutions proved to be only of limited suitability for use in schools. Currently, Free Software can be found in nearly all fields of application. Outstanding examples are the image processing software GIMP and the HTML editor asWedit.

The use of Free Software replacing standard software

packages, however, has not yet won. This can be attributed to the still not fully developed graphical user interface KDE and of course to the monopoly of Microsoft.

The barrier to changing sides in this case is due to the worldwide standardized *Office* software packages, which can be seen as a kind of "confidence-building" measure when looking at the new learning, working, and living demands imposed on individuals by the information society.

The main goal of basic computer training in schools, however, is not "user training" for software packages but the acquisition of problem-solving strategies for an appropriate use in the respective school subjects. A valuable insight, gained partially from my own long-term experience as multimedia workshop trainer, is the general openness and curiosity prevailing among youths to leave the customary paths of "usability". Feelings of insecurity and reservations about abandoning repetitive user habits are seen mainly among the teaching staff, for instance if familiar user routines – like opening and closing of text documents (.doc) – don't work anymore.

But Open Source within the field of education also means the fundamental question if and to what extent today's educational system can meet the requirements of an increasingly computerized and mediatized teaching and learning culture organizationally and curricularly. Seymour Papert, one of the most ardent advocates of computer-assisted learning environments, sees the actual potential in children's discovery-based learning outside of school, which is usually impeded by schools. Papert's vision of the computer as "knowledge machine", which allows children to explore undreamt-of new worlds, are based on his theory of constructionism. This theory says that, in the context of learning processes, learners should be motivated as often as possible to jointly negotiate a product or to individually carry out processes of knowledge construction (see Papert 1993, 143).

An open learning environment therefore requires measures to intensively reduce bureaucracy in educational institutions and to open them up to the outside. According to Papert, entering a "new era of learning" will only become possible once, apart from technical aspects, social arrangements are also taken into account: e.g. greater involvement of parents, teachers and students in decision-making processes, support of unconventional teaching and learning methods.

Looking at the concept of Open Source and the resulting "gift culture" it is necessary to determine to what extent this model is transferable to freely accessible knowledge sources that can actually be "patched". Commercial knowledge providers, which by now are increasingly present in European countries – formerly educational publishers and the alliance of IT corporations with scientific experts – do not only challenge the hitherto existing educational system, but raise the general question if and to what extent school as a state institution can continue to exist in the upcoming "knowledge war".

The simple accumulation of knowledge does not suffice to fulfill schools' comprehensive educational mission.

Within educational discourse this is mentioned, and rightly so, when reproaching the educational system for its lack of innovative energy. Innovative capability cannot be reduced down to only the acquisition of technical knowledge nor to the free availability of knowledge resources in networks.

The model of a virtual school, and therefore also the model of *kunstnetzwerk*, is part of a process of change within schools, which has to be viewed within the framework of a fundamental change in society. The development of new media is accompanied by possibilities to quickly record, process, save and transfer great quantities of data in diverse modes of representation. These possibilities are going to bring forth enormous qualitative changes in the fields of building, organizing, and socially opening up bodies of knowledge as well as in the field of communication between individuals, groups and political decision-makers. The technical processing of such data, however, can only unfold its productive potential as part of social communication and agreement/understanding processes.

At the same time, the scope for action and development of individuals is profoundly influenced by the access and user options connected with ICT. In this context it needs to be particularly taken into account that social processes and individual behavior patterns themselves can become the object of automated data processing by way of recording personal data. Boris Groys (2000) refers to a media-ontological suspicious fact, which is structurally not comprehensible for people concentrating on examining the medial interface. This suspicious fact describes what a so-called

37
Open Systems, 2010.
Infographics

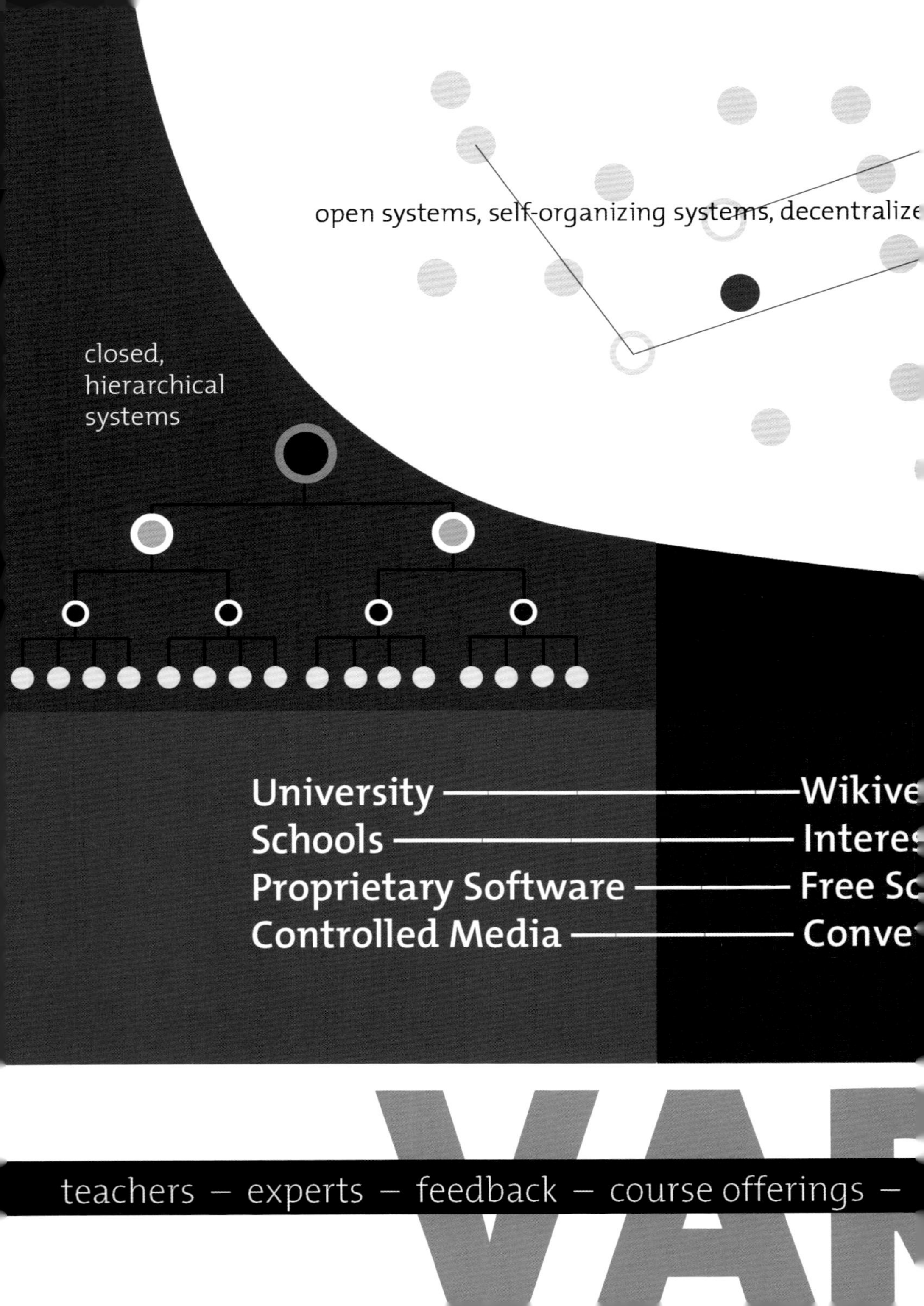
open systems, self-organizing systems, decentralize
closed, hierarchical systems
University —— Wikive
Schools —— Interes
Proprietary Software —— Free Sc
Controlled Media —— Conve
VAR
teachers – experts – feedback – course offerings –

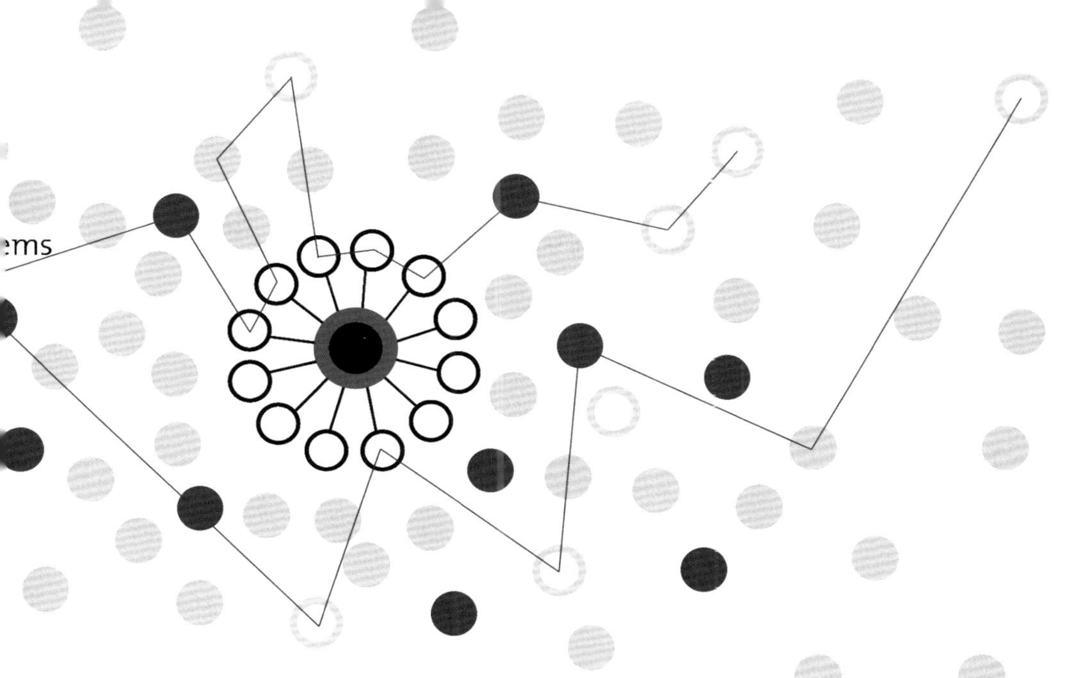

, Community of Practices
oups, Social Networks
re
onal media

IETY

ng times – learning materials – customization

"netizen" feels regarding interaction on the web, which can be intuitively sensed but ultimately not understood. Each interaction on the web harbors the risk of a demographic analysis in the background, which appraises the user's personal affinities, attitudes and preferences – and which addresses a potential, and certainly surprised, consumer with the next bulk mail.

The enormous potential of communicative and informative potential lying within the European and Austrian virtual school is leading it – unlike the commercial suppliers, which have to concentrate on ever more elaborate interaction mechanisms for conveying learning content via multimedia – towards the development of platforms that intend to enhance the transition from a receptive to a participative understanding of mediality.

I consider the increasing willingness of IT officers/managers at educational institutions to adopt the Linux model as an important and necessary reaction to the hard- and software spiral.

A look at the mass media reveals that Linux has long turned into a serious alternative when procuring an operating system. Our offer shall encourage disseminators at schools to give the students an understanding of the diversity among operating systems. This is how a Linux distributor explains his company's commitment. He mentions the mainly free applications as one of the many advantages of employing Linux in schools. Due to its economical use of hardware resources, employing Linux allows schools, which often have a low budget for IT equipment, to put even older computers to good use. "Why Linux" points out a multitude of possibilities that allow schools to access the wide pallet of Linux applications even with the aid of support free of charge.

Some of the most important points for use in schools is the fact that Linux is a real multi-user and multi-tasking network operating system, in which multi-user and multi-tasking applications work without time lag. It is designed and highly suitable for server, router, firewall and desktop use as a standard. There is no difference between server and desktop systems. Due to its stringent allocation of access rights, it is nearly impossible for students to damage the system.

With Linux, the use of external (e.g. older computers) and virtual terminals is built in from the outset as a standard.

It includes as a standard all tools for internet connections and for intranet setup: WWW server, proxy, mail, and news server. Each distribution contains nearly everything you need for comprehensive network maintenance. As this is usually not the case for other operating systems, it makes Linux especially interesting for schools considering that additional software needs additional funds.

Linux is compatible with all platforms, no matter whether Windows, Apple or Novell, and can be implemented without problems in heterogeneous networks.

Along with the increasing number of users, the number of available programs is increasing as well. The non-profit association Free Software and Education, founded in 1999, aims at cooperation between educational institutions and companies that offer Open Source products for Linux or make their products available for use with Linux to the educational sector without license fees. Apart from its programmatic "open theory" platform, this Open School Server provides a multitude of services ranging from installation support and field reports of schools all the way to a complete Linux software suite.

Being able to deal with new ICTs is a basic requirement for coping with working life in the future. Processing data to obtain information and using this information for problem solving is a cultural technique that everybody needs to be able to manage with.

The imparting of cultural techniques and competencies should therefore concentrate on techniques that will dominate the students' future working life and that ideally should play a role in all school subjects.

Thus, schools are increasingly considered as market generators, as locations in which the foundations for computer and internet literacy are laid to provide for the success of those markets expected to bring forth new stimuli for economic growth and employment, especially in the services sector.

Essential parts of our social reality are reconstructed by way of software. The dominance of individual software producers like Microsoft makes the users not only blind to possible alternatives, but also suggests controllability and thus competency through standardizing formalized ways of communication in diverse fields of activity.

"We believe in technology's ability to preserve what is

best in higher education – we also know that our survival as a company depends on your success in creating thinkers, problem solvers, and global citizens. In this age of instant global information, the skills, values and capacities fostered by higher education have never been more important. You know education. We know technology. Working together, we can harness the benefits of these exciting new technologies to meet the educational needs of the 21st century market place". (Gates 1999)

But what would happen if school communities did not encounter the technology-oriented computer industry as a "critical mass" but as a community of "critical users"? The potential represented by the schools of Europe or even worldwide not as a market but as a community of interest could start a completely new form of resource allocation in the sense of an Open Source movement – and I am deliberately not saying industry that would comply with the requirements of this community for ICT in the form of teaching and learning media.

School still means the enhancement of consciousness and cannot content itself with the simple operating of standard software. One part of education necessarily comprises the learning of cultural techniques. Free Software, I find, creates an informational free space. Free Software being accessible to everybody and the creation of space that is independent of commercial interests with its help are crucial in this respect. In the light of increasing tendencies towards commercialization of education, this free space for the field of education appears especially important.

The democratic values of Open Source culture not only initiated entrepreneurial rethinking processes – by now even traditional companies like IBM have adapted their practices successfully to this new culture – but also raised the question to what extent this movement is able to influence the general cultural, political and other development of a global society. Jean-Claude Guedon, OC member of the internet Society (ISOC) – one of the most important non-profit internet organizations – emphasized at the *Inet 2000* conference that an Open Source culture is able to shift general culture from an individual, possessive production of knowledge to a dynamical, community-driven one. This means that people can begin to compile school books or compose music jointly.

Ingrid Lohmann (1998) however has observed increased tendencies towards commercialization in current educational discourse, assuming a commercialization of access to information, its turning into goods. "Not individuals will own their knowledge, but the company that employs them. The concept of education will irrevocably belong to the past" (ibid. p.1). Lohmann assumes that, contrary to Luhmann's seemingly apodictic statement "what we know about our society, even about the world we live in, we know via mass media" (Luhmann 1996, 9), our knowledge about the world is constituted – also and mainly – through the educational and academic system. "By posting contents on the electronic networks (content providing), however, a genuine field for educational processes in the sense of Comenius could develop," Lohmann assumes.

In his presentation on the subject "Science as Open Source

process," Friedrich Kittler emphasizes "that the freedom/liberty of academia hinges on the freedom/liberty of source codes". Kittler equates academia with the university "without wanting to put forward too much vested interest". It is part and parcel of universities, he argues, that the knowledge generated by them, contrary to that of closed or secret research centers, has to be able to circulate without the protection of patents or copyrights.

Due to the technical reproducibility of information, the universal Turing machine now allows the differences, the boundaries established by media technology, between technical, scientific and cultural knowledge to fade away.

The fight between faculties as once described by Kant might be solved peacefully, simply because there are no longer books standing against laboratories standing against councils in the different faculties, but all knowledge, also the cultural, is being processed in computers. It seems to me that this offers the Open Sources and free operating systems a major opportunity.

(Vienna, 2000; translated by Judith Keinath)

38
Untitled,
1995.
Color copy, plexiglass, wood, 105 x 72 x 6 cm

2

photography multimedia

39
Seoul #12,
2008.
Color print,
31.8 x 47.3 cm

산부인
종로
의 문화재 지도

40
Seoul #18,
2008.
Color print,
31.8 x 47.3 cm

NTERNET
(Brodband)

41
India #5, detail,
2009.
Color print,
31.8 x 47.3 cm

42
India #6, detail,
2009.
Color print,
31.8 x 47.3 cm

43
India #7, detail,
2009.
Color print,
31.8 x 47.3 cm

44
India #18,
detail, 2008.
Color print,
31.8 x 47.3 cm

QUICKTIME VR Navigation
NODES
TIMELINE

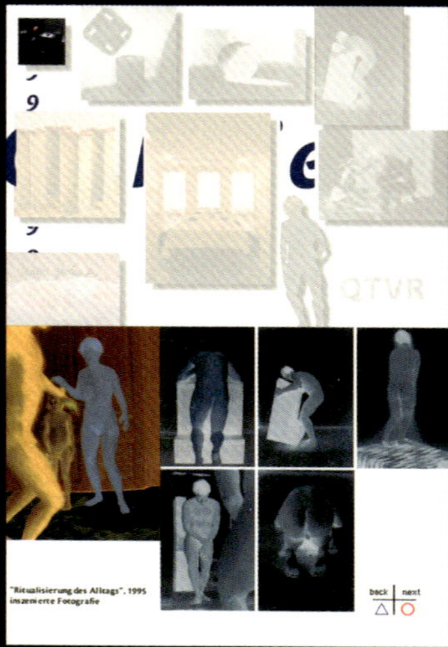

91 92 93 94 95 96 97

45
Screen-, navigation-design of the interactive CD-Rom *Stefan Sonvilla-Weiss Arbeiten 1991–1997*

46
Borromini Interactive, 1999. Flash game design

BORROMINI INTERACTIVE (1999)

Screenshots from the interactive online learning game *Borromini interactive*. Design and programming of this Flash based online game (420 kb) for the Virtual Albertina Vienna in 1999.
Virtual Albertina is a project of the Austrian National Collection of Graphic Art Albertina, Vienna. It is a museum of expanded opportunities, of participation, interaction, and interdisciplinary focus. The target group of Virtual Albertina are teachers and students who, in a joint effort, should help to eliminate boundaries between the museum and its visitors by means of new communication technologies. Students and teachers are encouraged to develop projects related to the subject matter of Albertina exhibitions, which are then going to be presented in the World Wide Web and in the exhibitions themselves.

The interactive learning game has been designed for teachers, students and people interested in art.
The game is divided into three parts:

1. The architecture of Francesco Borromini
2. Biography
3. Baroque living

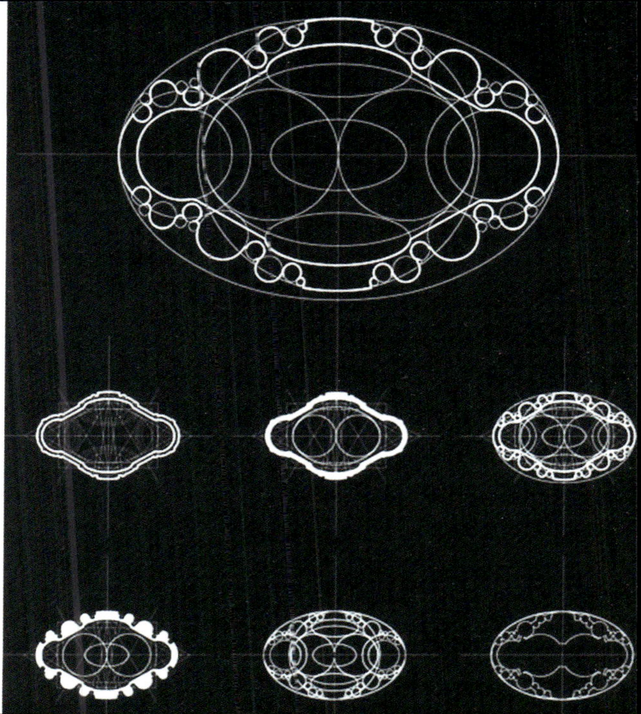

um 1620:
er zeichnet
und studiert
die römische
Antike und
den Bau zu
St.Peter.

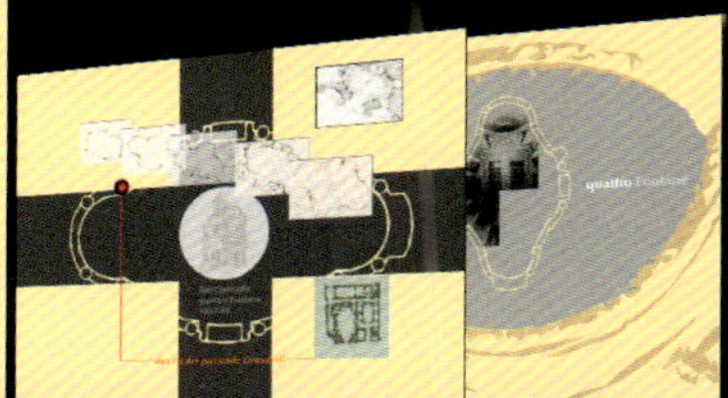

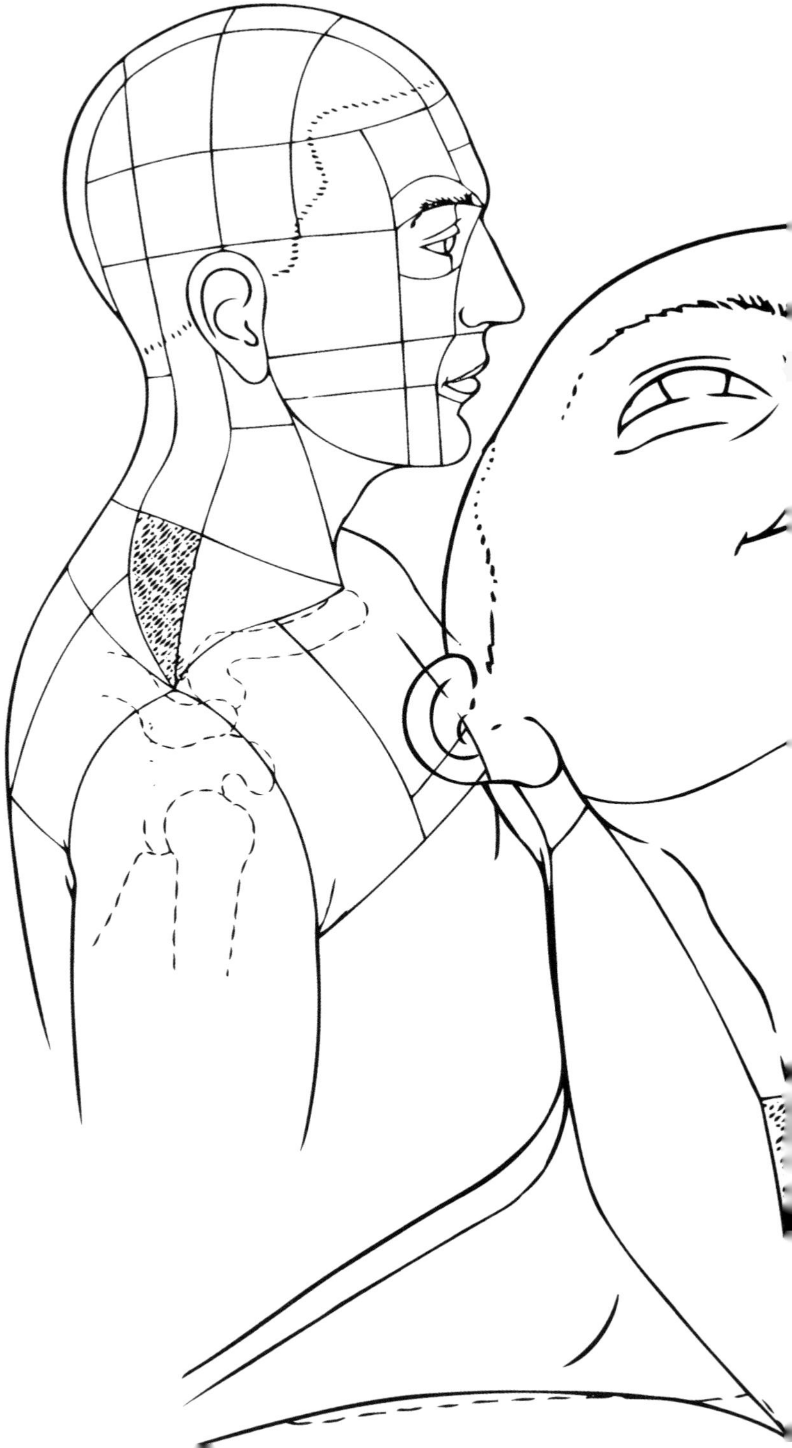

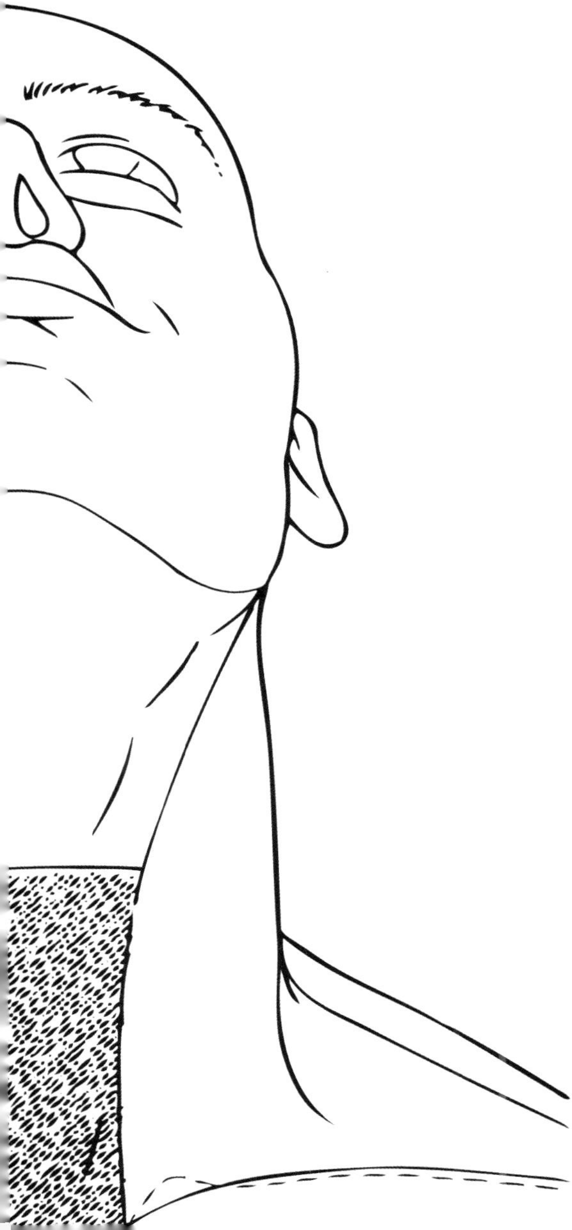

47
Bach, Animated drawings, 1994.

48
Stills from the animation *Fruits,* 1997.

49
Body-Fruits, 1997.
Drawing, photography, 840 x 594 mm

50
Land, 1993.
Color print, transparency film, 840 x 594 mm

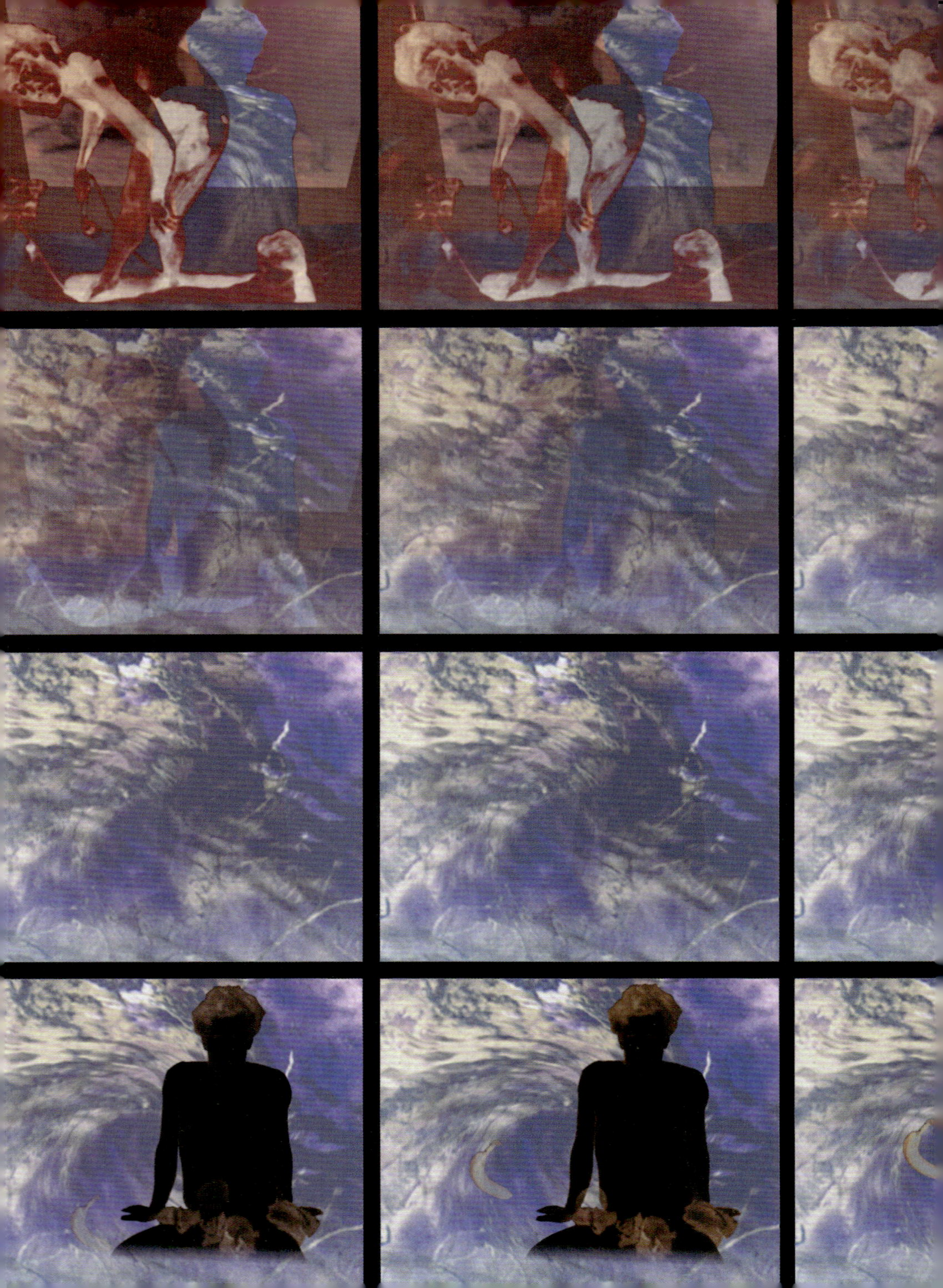

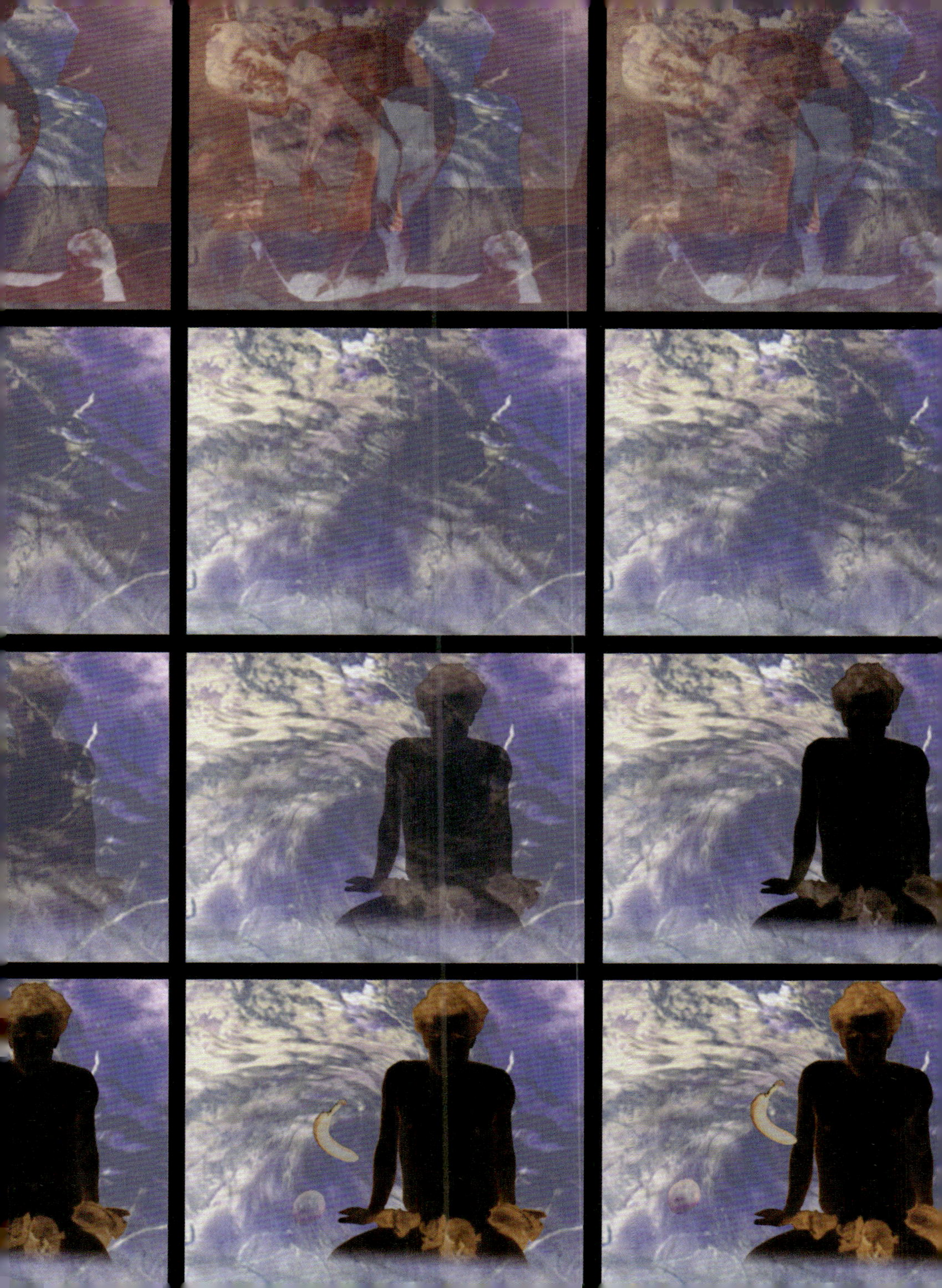

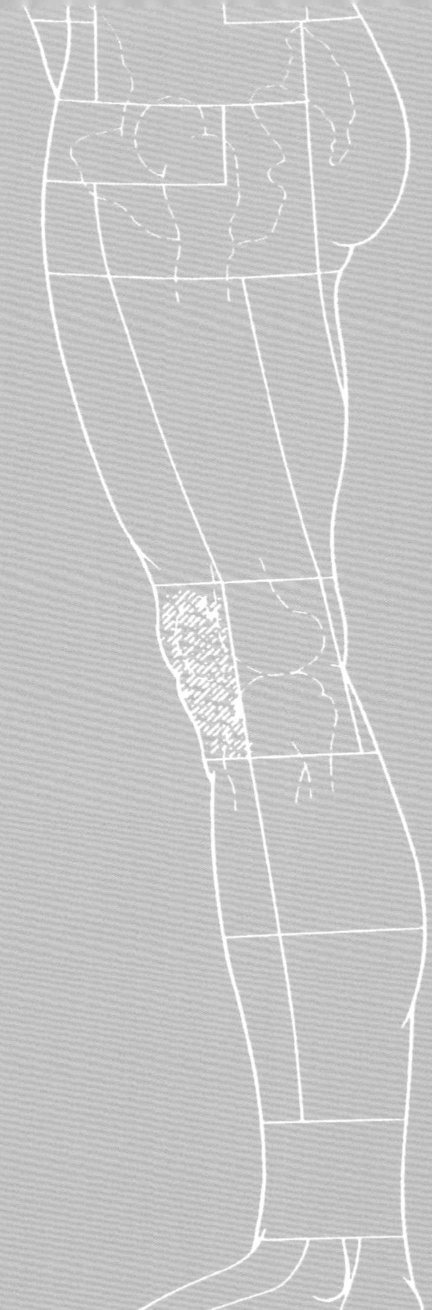

51
Untitled, 1997.
Computer-aided large scale imagery, 120 x 80 cm

52
Detail from the photo series *Fruits*, 1993.

53
Stills from the animation *Morphing,* 1997

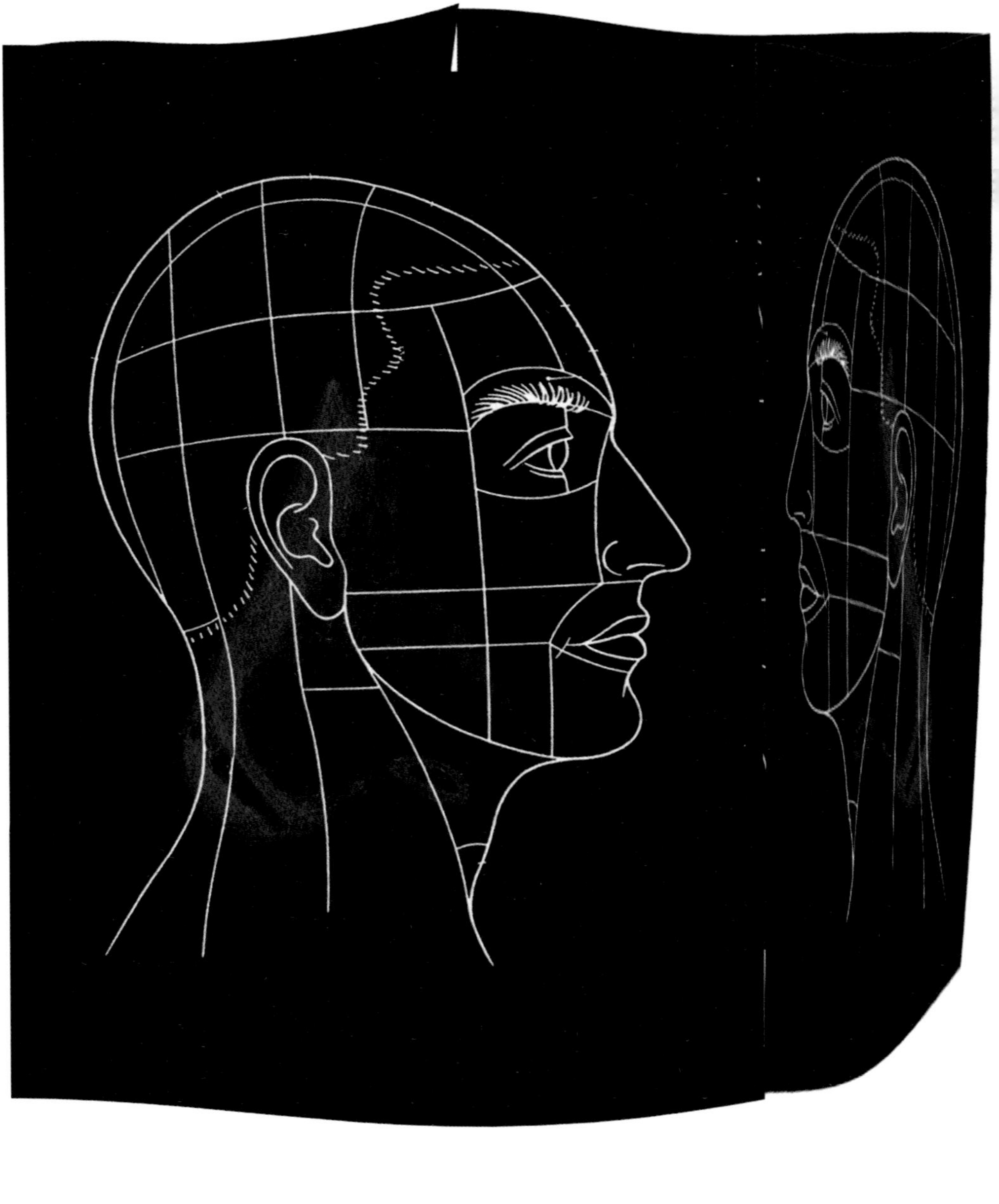

54
Healing, 1994.
Mixed media,
installation view,
Vienna

55
Detail of *Flying Bodies,* 1994.
Transparency
film

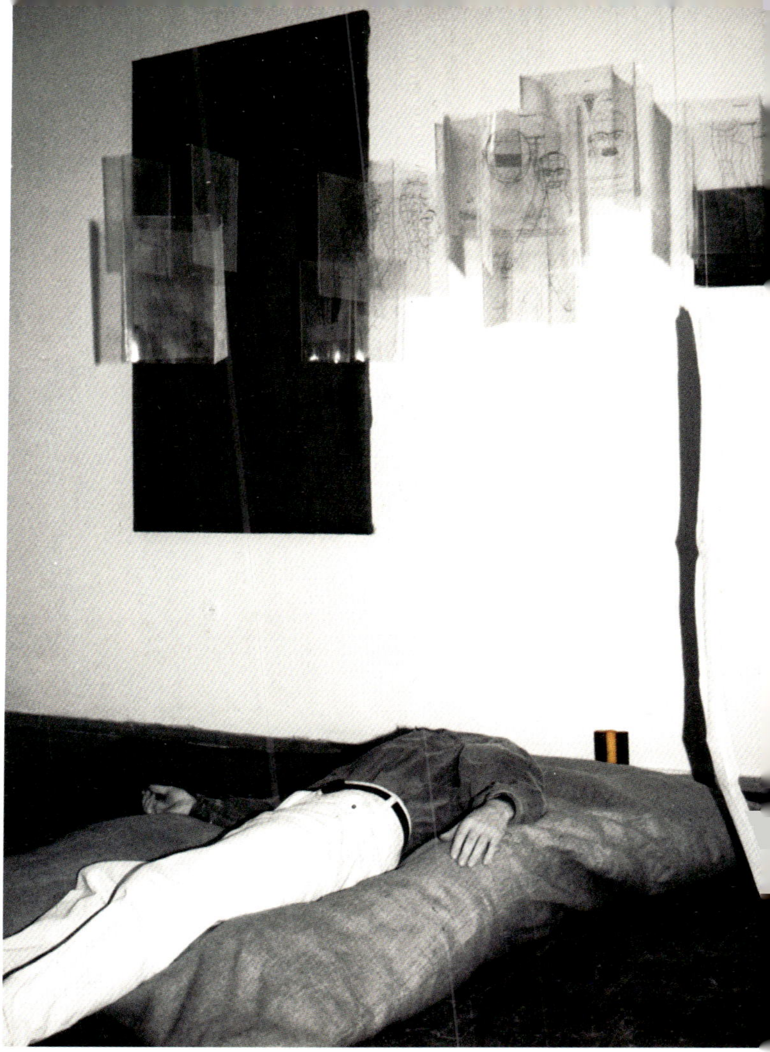

56
Trafik, *1997.*
Exhibition view
art gallery
Szombathely

57
Family rituals,
1993
Photo objects,
240 x 120 x
6 cm

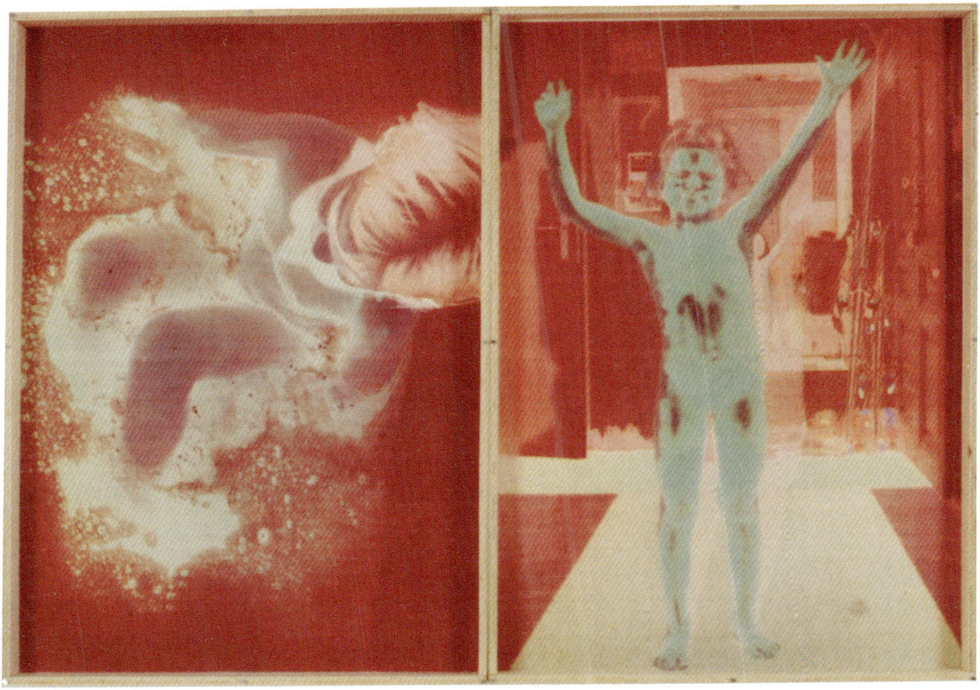

58
Feli, 1993.
Photo objects,
140 x 100 x
6 cm

59
Self-Portrait,
1992.

60
Untitled,
1993. Color print, 21 x 15 cm

3

installations exhibitions

THE SIMPLICITY AND JOY OF BEING (EINFACH SEIN)

In 1993 I worked for an ecological food co-operative called *Der Gemüsebote* (The Vegetable Carrier) in Vienna to make a living as an artist. Everything there was bottom-up, simple, organic, enthusiastic and cooperative, driven by the impulse to do something better for society.

On a side note, the company logo came from Stefan Sagmeister shortly before he started to form the New York-based Sagmeister Inc. in 1993.

61
Einfach Sein,
Exhibition
invitation card,
1993.
Gallery 5020
Salzburg

People from various backgrounds shared the same passion for basic democratic principles and fair trade. We are naturally inclined to idealize past experiences, yet today's quest to break with existing economic principles and value systems that are entirely based on accumulation of commodities made possible by exploiting natural and human resources affirm the importance of this small initiative.

Even though the life cycle of the cooperative was short, the work done was not in vain, as marketing cooperatives and associations of producers offering organic products directly to consumers proliferated significantly in the following years. The concept behind this organic farming-driven approach was somewhat seminal and simple at the same time: to support local farmers and to market and sell their organic food to Viennese households via a direct delivery

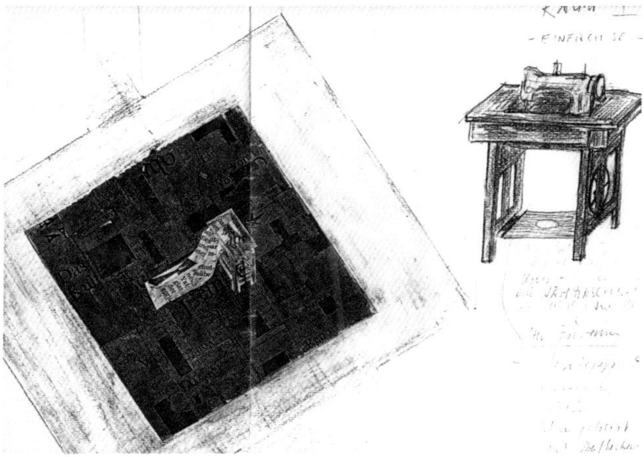

62
Sketches of the *working room*, 1993. Collage, drawing on paper; 297 x 420 mm

63
Detail view of the *working room*, 1993. Sewing machine, wooden box, newspaper carpet

service. Customers could directly order and configure their organic vegetable boxes and food. Orders were made by phone or fax at that time. Computers were rare and solely deployed for bookkeeping, calculation and inventory. In retrospect it was a rather peculiar encounter of idiosyncratic individuals who shared a passion for alternative paths of living and working.

Still memorable and from the perspective of today's economic crises it is rather appealing that I partly got compensated for my work in natural goods instead of money.

Nowadays Web 2.0 generation remediates open source and peer-to-peer production principles in various exchange and value-based forms, in co-designing a product through shared expertise and resources; bartering of material and immaterial goods; reciprocal provision of time, skills, tools and expertise; design ideas and concepts in exchange with production of re- and up-cycled materials and goods, amongst other examples. When I started to conceive of the exhibition at the gallery space in Salzburg in 1992 I remember that one of my main intentions was to investigate conditions of work and labor, re-creation and community in the form of a creative and experimental approach through a performative, interactive and communicative encounter.

The materials I used to work with for the installation in the gallery space were reminiscent of the poor materials used in arte povera. So I forced myself to see what was available in the immediate surroundings, how I could reuse and repurpose existing materials, goods and objects that were uselessly lying around in my living space and studio.

Almost all the "ingredients" were second-hand, used, and repurposed into artefacts, useful and useless objects that substantially informed the interactive design processes. The fruit boxes were adjusted as seating; newspapers were colored, impregnated and sewed together to form a carpet; pigments were used to rub the wall.

64
Installation view of the ***working room***, 1993, Mixed media; 4 x 4 m

The concept of space I had in mind took up the limitations and possibilities of the gallery space entailing the challenge to intersect three different concepts of living, working and meditating as an unified concept and stimulating interactive visitor experiences at the same time. On entering the exhibition space the visitors were confronted with the first installation assembled of an old sewing machine, a fruit box as seating in front of it, standing on a 4-square-meter carpet made of newspapers.

In approaching the unknown technical territory of the old sewing machine's mechanics vague memories from my

childhood popped up on how to employ the treadle and to guide the thread down the front of the sewing machine to the left of the tension discs. Then you need to pull it around the bottom and up. Here are a few more iterative steps that would help you to get this old sewing machine working, which I reconstructed with the help of some vintage documents available on the web:

> *Bring the thread from the front of the machine toward the back and through the loop, which is usually on a lever that moves up and down. This lever is located on the front or side of the antique Singer sewing machines.*
>
> *Gently pull the thread down through the spiral guide. This guide is usually to the upper left of the needle, and it can be located on the machine body or right above the needle.*
>
> *Thread the needle. It is helpful to trim the thread right before threading to cut off any frayed ends, leaving a blunt end that is easier to thread. If your vision is not perfect, use a needle threader by inserting the threader into the needle, putting the thread through the needle threader loop, and then pulling the needle threader back through the machine needle.*

65
Installation view of the *dining room*, 1993.

The living room was designed as a space for a communicative encounter around a dining table where simple bowls contained fruit to eat or to take away. Wooden boxes standing upright with crafted pillars on top accommodated the audience as an inviting gesture to sit down for contemplation, eating, reading, working and discussion.

The wall painting was conceived as a participatory artwork in the form of a site-spanning frieze containing simple fruit symbols that could be stamped on the wall. I later

learned from the gallery owner that over the course of time most of the visitors lost their timidity to engage with the interactive and co-creative concept of the artwork.

Today many young artists and designers are seeking sustainable, energy-neutral and ecologically friendly solutions to break through the barriers and walls of predominant mass industrial production. The goal is to create a state of equilibrium between taking and giving back resources.

Our global economy is based on scarcity, which is based on supply (how much there is available) and demand (how much people want it). The more demand and less supply, the more scarcity. Since the economy is about managing scarcity, economic scarcity is a necessary component. In fact, plentiful commodities are not considered something you can make much money with. They are not valued as much as something that has real or perceived scarcity.

66
Installation view of the *sleeping room*, 1993. Pigments, jute, wooden pallet

The scarcity-based economy is collapsing and people are starting to wake up to the idea that something else needs to happen.

While I am trying to weave my thoughts into the blueish pigmented walls of the sleeping room the here and now coalesces with my imagination and dreams of a brighter world. What if we ran our economy not on this principle of scarcity, but on the principle of abundance?

Ironically, this tragedy is self-made because people eagerly embrace the myth of scarcity with respect to everything that in reality is or could be abundant if we used our imagination, and they ignore the one thing that is actually running out for humanity.

CHILDREN'S PLAYGROUND

It's almost impossible to look back into history without distorted images. In this case I am the archivist, the image creator, the author of the artwork who after almost 20 years tries to assemble broken memories with notes and sketches from the past that help me to see what is in front of my eyes. Undoubtedly the 6x6 cm Ektachromes taken with a Hasselblad are perfectly preserved and depict the artwork in unrivalled quality. Some of the pieces making up the installation are stored in my studio in Vienna; others were sold and will probably hang or stand in private or public collections.

67
Installation view *Children's Playground,* 1993.

68
Children's Playground #1, 1993.
Mixed media, 100 X 40 X 40 cm

Two of the smaller liquid diaries (acrylic boxes filled with synthetic liquids, a mix of materials and garbage) are in close proximity to my current home in Vantaa, Finland. From this immediate experience of getting a hold of the "real" object I attempt to find Ariadne's thread.

In fact, the children's playground was an installation. The vintage rocking horse is kept in storage, the plastic bathtube is filled with concrete containing an acrylic paned box filled with synthetic liquids and a plastic toy goldfish. A frozen world of artifacts, reminiscent of vivid use, joy and play, marks out an irrevocable loss, but of what?

Toys will be used and locked away once the kids get bored and have grown out of their clothes. My daughter used to collect a vast amount of plush toys which either got lost or were drastically reduced during our several relocations in Vienna and later move to Brussels and Helsinki. I wonder

what happens to all the private assortments of toys when they are out of use. The idea of this installation was not primarily grounded in any kind of recycling initative; rather, in hindsight there were a multitude of content-, material-, form-related issues to be discovered and experimented with, eventually leading to unprecedented aesthetic objects that gradually developed into a gallery installation.

After four years of intense contention with all sorts of cardboards, a lightweight material I used for constructing three-dimensional wall objects, I started to experiment with liquids and acrylic sheets to construct containers that could be shaken and re-arranged in different shapes and modular configurations. To avoid the container becoming misted up I had to search for synthetic liquids that would not vaporize. What interested me was the combination of different materials, for example pigments, plaster, photographs, fax images and garbage with synthetic fluids and to find out how these materials reacted in combination. Once these boxes were filled and tested for impermeability one could turn them around and wait and see what new kinds of images arose out of this interaction.

69
Liquid Diaries, 1993.
Mixed media, 200 X 40 X 15 cm

These objects, which I call *liquid diaries,* have been in use for 17 years, and, surprisingly, the color quality of the liquids have not faded, nor has the wide range of materials that were enclosed changed much in character.

It seems as if they would stand metaphorically for the many explosive time capsules humankind has produced in the form of contaminated radioactive waste bombs encased in concrete and dumped into the sea.

70
Alphabet,
1993.
Ink, wood stain, varnish on panels,
240 X 40 cm

71
Children's Playground #2,
1993.
Mixed media,
200 X 45 X 45 cm

72
Children's Playground #3,
1993.
Mixed media,
140 X 60 X 70 cm

The four plaster ducks came out of a plastic mold that was originally a toy duck. Surrounded by floating plaster tires covered with red wax the duck's territory was clearly demarcated; they were safe yet imprisoned. A bluish inflatable canoe, non-repairable though beautiful in shape and color, is spread out on granulated foam plastic and encoated by a construction made of wood and acrylic sheet. Today the object stands in the same upright position as it is depicted in the installation view from 1993 in a public collection. Has anyone ever thought about moving the object around, clockwise horizontally, or mounting it on a wall?

73
Children's Playground #4, 1993.
Mixed media, 120 X 45 X 45 cm

74
Children's Playground #5, 1993
Mixed media, 140 X 60 X 70 cm

In discovering new territories of playful experiment with mixed media, (re)appropriation of new and old production techniques and technologies my horizon widened by way of learning to understand and getting to know the materials' inherent limitations and possibilities to create something new. I set myself a few parameters for orientation and organization of consecutive design steps that were rather experienced as essential completion of certain tasks than restrictions.

Prior to the making my studio turned into a laboratory of ideation, probing and narration in which each little thing incorporated a different story. That's the moment to immerse in and to listen to the things around you, a moment of unintentional playfulness ...

75
Children's Playground #8, 1993.
Detail view

LIBERTY, FOR THE DEMOCRAT, CONSISTS NOT IN BEING ABLE TO SAY EVERYTHING HE THINKS, BUT IN NOT HAVING TO THINK ABOUT EVERYTHING HE SAYS

Davila's aphorism stayed with me for quite a long time, and in retrospect, going back in history (more than 20 years) I recall George Steiner's *In Bluebeard's Castle: Some Notes Towards the Redefinition of Culture* as the inspiring source containing Davila's statement.

76
Studio view,
Vienna, 1994.

Taking this multilayered language game further the essence of the sentence becomes clearer and clearer the more you repeat and reflect on the freedom of speech, unfiltered and uncensored information in the realm of public communication and discourse.

However, unfettered vox populi has unleashed populist moves towards a radicalization of verbal expression in amplifying rudimentary instincts of anger and agony as a dividing means to respond to existing conflicts in multicultural societies. Numerous examples of right-wing movements and demagogues across Europe underpin sadly enough this presupposition. The media controls and impacts creating of public opinion.

The hegemony of media tycoons across the globe has an equivalent in former Silicon Valley start-ups which

77
Synthetic Kneelers,
1991.
Mixed media, 100 X 110 X 35 cm. Exhibition view, Contemporary Art Space Vienna

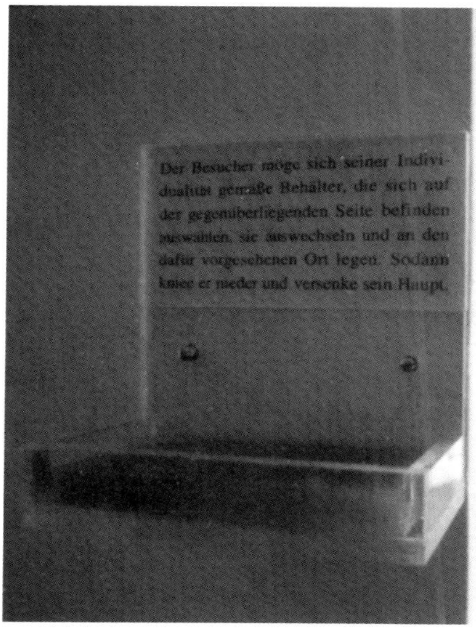

78
Instructions,
1991.
Mixed media, 25 X 10 X 25 cm. Exhibition view

subsequently dominated the western world by searching, sharing and exploiting private information that people voluntarily give away to make themselves visible to the rest of the world. The degree of separation and alienation people suffer in their private and daily life routines equates with the degree of desire for potentially infinite spaces of possibility, the virtual – which naturally clashes with the factual (in what is called cognitive dissonance). On the other hand the course of the world by necessity is unstoppable, and the question is whether the "Arab Spring" revolutions pursued democratic goals at first by civil engagement through participatory media – something that at least the western media promulgates.

79
Installation View, 1991. Contemporary Art Space Vienna

Or did the "hard facts" of a society in which the youth had no future at all inevitably call for unparalleled change, which nevertheless developed into different directions than the Western democracies had in mind?

At the time the idea for this installation emerged there was no internet or WWW around. TV, radio and newspapers and magazines were the prevalent communication and information media. In the art world interactive installations in the form of user engagement with the object still incorporated insurmountable barriers to tangible experiences with the artwork.

It seemed to me a logical consequence to develop further the co-creating aspects of the viewer-object relationship towards haptic and participatory practices in which the viewer becomes a user and part of the artwork. On completion of my solid fibreboard series the time was ripe to

80
Liquid Boxes,
1991.
Contemporary
Art Space
Vienna

explore something new. Luckily the same company from which I ordered fibreboard in great quantities provided me with a new packaging material made of polyethylene foam available in 300 x 50 x 5 cm panels. From there I started to expand the scope of investigation and experimentation in the direction of hitherto unknown territories to produce usable design objects. What played to my advantage was the extremely lightweight and effortlessly workable material, which could be easily cut and joined together with a special adhesive. After having collected a sound understanding of the technical components through combination and fusion of different, purely synthetic media the making of three-dimensional large sculptures became possible.

I remember how I felt when kneeling for the first time on

a foam kneeler. Since the material was so soft and warming kneeling became an act of joy rather than a haunting torture on plain wood. The prayer book was replaced by two acrylic boxes filled with dishwashing liquids, shampoos or softeners and were discharged into the material so that a seamless intersection of both materials created a plain surface.

Following the instructions in the gallery space, the visitor was invited to pick up one of the liquid reservoirs and to replace it with one of the preconfigured boxes in the kneelers. The gallery space was permeated with a penetrating synthetic odor that came from a small wall bin filled with dish detergent. What appeared to be a contemplative space from the standpoint of a pedestrian's glimpse through the window in fact drastically diverged with the concept behind the scenes.

On entering the small exhibition space the primary sense experience was caused by the obtrusive smell of synthetic liquids from the small acrylic reservoir mounted on the wall close to the entrance. There you could also read the installation instructions, which officially permitted the visitor to interact with the art objects. Next to it was mounted an acrylic shelf on which four similar boxes sat filled with red, blue, yellow and white synthetic liquids. By following the instructions, the visitor could make his choice of picking them up and replacing them with the ones embedded in the kneelers.

In hindsight I am not quite sure whether these instructions made people feel more engaged with the artwork.

Rather, it was my wishful thinking that this little intervention could smoothen the boundaries between the auratic and interactive space.

The installation was quickly arranged as the components were of manageable scope and easily transportable by car. What better material could be used for transportation than the foam packaging material of which the kneelers were made. The size and volume of these objects were measured exactly and adjusted in spatial proportion to the volume of the exhibition space. At the end 4 kneelers containing two liquid boxes each were placed in a row on a black covered floating screed.

81
Installation piece, 1991. Studio view Vienna

Ironically, the freedom of choice to unrestrictedly move around the colorful liquid boxes and replace them with each other was not transferred to the hierarchical order of the black polyethylene foam objects. The imaginable space of possibilities is that of individual choices, which could be altered whenever a new impulse directs the attention to new directions.

Closing time. The space, the liquids and the artwork has been emptied; later on somewhere in the city unidentifiable residues of a strange smelling and looking material were found.

> *Situations give rise to measurements,*
> *measurements give rise to estimates,*
> *estimates give rise to analysis,*
> *analysis give rise to balancing,*
> *balance gives rise to triumph.*
> Sun Tzu

NEW YORK, NEW YORK

This was my first New York trip by invitation of a gallerist with whom I explored the cityscape for two weeks in the early autumn of 1991. The black-and-white shots capture some of my 24-hour wanderings up and down Manhattan and Brooklyn. I plugged into the city's nervous system from the moment I arrived at JFK airport until I left.

Back in my studio I used some of the photographs for further experimentation. This led to acrylic wall objects filled with synthetic liquids, black pigments and screen printing on transparency film. By shaking the objects the pigments temporarily emulsified with the liquids and then bit by bit demulsified and fell to the ground. This autopoetic painting process could take a few days depending on the intensity of shaking and blending of the two elements. Each time the interaction with the art piece created anew unexpected and contingent transmutations. The longer you wait the clearer the picture becomes.

82
New York #7,
1991.
Photograph

In my ear still resonates *Grandmaster Flash and* the *Furious Five* ... and, there is nothing more to say.

Ah New York New York big city of dreams
And everything in New York ain't always what it seems
You might get fooled if you come from out of town
But I'm down by law and I know my way around
Too much too many people, too much -- a ha hah
Too much, too many people, too much, rrrrrrrah!

A castle in the sky, one mile high
Built to shelter the rich and greedy
Rows of eyes, disguised as windows
Looking DOWN on the poor and the needy
Miles of people, marchin-up the avenue
Doing what they gotta do, just to get by
I'm living in the land of plenty and many
But I'm damn sure poor and I don't know why

Too much, ah too many people, too much
Too much, too many people, too much!

A man's on a ledge, says he's gonna jump
People gather round, said, "He won't he's just a chump"
Cause he lost his job, then he got robbed
His mortgage is due and his marriage is through
He says he ain't gonna pay no child support
Because the bitch left him without a second thought
He got nothing to eat, no shoes on his feet
She even left his clothes out in the street
He keeps hearing noises when he's at home
He always hears voices when he's all alone
His wife took the kids, the car and the crib
In this man's world, so much for women's lib

83
New York #14, 1991.
Photograph

New York New York big city of dreams
But everything in New York ain't always what it seems
You might get fooled if you come from out of town
But I'm down by law, and I know my way around

Down in the Village, you might think I'm silly
but you can't tell the women from the men sometimes
They're sugar and spice and everything nice
But when you get 'em home ain't no telling what you find
Right next door is a little old man
I seen him eating dog food out of a can
He says, "I got to eat, when I can't afford meat
I barely can stand, on my own two feet"

AREA
Lofts
Stores
Offices
Famous
Clothing
JOY-LUD

I got a bad habit and I just can't break it
Somethin's on my mind and I just can't shake it
I need some time, and I want some space
I gotta get away from the human race

Too much, ah too many people, too much... a-ha hah
Too much, ah too many people, too much! Rrrrrrah!

Staring at a skyscraper reachin into heaven
When over in the ghetto I'm livin in hell
Just play ball or be an entertainer
cause niggaz like me can't read too well
Nobody loves me, nobody cares
I dreamed about a life but I'm livin in a nightmare
Paranoid schizo, set back, snowbound
Bad news psycho, heart attack, breakdown!

Hee, huh (16X) HUH!
If only I could sleep just ten more minutes
I might find the strength to make another day
If I didn't have to get up, and do my thing
I would probably sleep my whole life away
I messed up a nice dream, somethin bout ice cream
Whipped cream fruits and a cherry on top
Now I gotta get up and face the world, huh
The pressure is on it ain't never gonna stop
I sho' gotta learn to use my mind
I don't wanna be kissin nobody's behind
Just standin on line lookin like a jerk
Gotta get off my butt and do a full day's work
I ran into a pothole, got into a car crash
Shoulda been thinkin and tried to fake whiplash
A crowd gathered round, they're callin me fat
Who you lookin at wit a face like that?

New York New York big city of dreams
Everything in New York ain't always what it seems
You might get fooled if you come from out of town

But I'm down by law and I know my way around
On 42nd Street, lookin for some action ...

84
New York Diaries,
1991-1992.
Foilprint, liquids, plexiglass
40 x 80 x 15 cm

BOXES, WORDS AND CONTRADICTIONS

2.02 Objects are simple.
2.0201 Every statement about complexes can be resolved into a statement about their constituents and into the propositions that describe the complexes completely.
2.021 Objects make up the substance of the world. That is why they cannot be composite.
2.0211 If the world had no substance, then whether a proposition had sense would depend on whether another proposition was true.
2.0212 In that case we could not sketch any picture of the world (true or false).
2.022 It is obvious that an imagined world, however different it may be from the real one, must have something – a form – in common with it.
2.023 Objects are just what constitute this unalterable form.
2.0231 The substance of the world can only determine a form, and not any material properties. For it is only by means of propositions that material properties are represented--only by the configuration of objects that they are produced. (Ludwig Wittgenstein, *Tractatus Logico-Philosophicus,* p. 2)

85
Studio View, Vienna,1991.

86
Fractal Innocence (Fraktale Unschuld), 1990-1991. Installation view Haus Wittgenstein, solid fibreboard, varnish; 240 x 160 x 12 cm

The installation for my exhibition at the Wittgenstein house in Vienna in 1991 was made up of three parts. Each part contains one piece or more of a three-dimensional, solid fibreboard object. The solid fibreboard objects were made of precisely cut forms that were seamlessly glued together so as to form spatial objects.

At that time solid fibreboard was available as quadrate formats, 1.84m x 1.84m, in brown or grey and 3mm thickness. All these data and the list of orders from the solid fibreboard factory is still archived in a box together with a collection of planimetrical drawings on transparent paper that laid the basis for all my solid board objects. The transparent paper depict boxes in various shapes and in different parallel projections.

87
Insight (Erkenntnis), 1991. Installation view with the artist, Haus Wittgenstein, cardboard, varnish, mirror glas, 15 parts each 28,5 x 9 x 9 cm

88
Installation view, Haus Wittgenstein, 1991

In the next step the transparent paper was laid over the solid board in order to transfer the drawing from one medium to the other. So the overlapping of two plane surfaces would not cause data loss, I decided to apply the simple method of piercing dots with a needle at each single corner point through the paper onto the solid board.

This meticulous exercise required full concentration since the dots had to exactly correspond with the corner points of the drawing.

Why didn't I draw directly on the solid board's surface? Because the modular character of some of the bigger objects required duplicate copies.

After the dots were placed on the solid board they were linked together outlining a congruent form that was carved out with a Stanley knife.

One form could take a sharp, angulated and distorted perspective, for example depicting a box with an open lid (see Fig. 89).

But how to turn a carved form into a three-dimensional object?

Depending on the height of the object stripes of a specific

width were cut out and glued orthogonally as side parts along the outline of the planimetric surface. The challenge was to mitre two meeting side parts at a sharp angle in such a way that there was no seam visible after they were glued together.

Once the side parts were all fixed and glued along the outline the base area with side parts was turned over and glued on the exact duplicate of the base area.

The resulting multiangular corpuses had different dimensions in which the maximum size reached 3 meters in diameter. It took me more than one year to accomplish this work, a masterpiece composed of more than 1000 single pieces perfectly designed and constructed with no other material than solid fibreboard. This piece was quite fragile and was unfortunately destroyed during an exhibition transport.

89
Open Box #1, 1991. Installation view Haus Wittgenstein, solid fibreboard, varnish; 120 x 80 x 12 cm

As a result, the size of the working desk in my studio expanded as the formats grew bigger over time.

At that time my work much resembled that of an architect. From 1988 onwards over a period of three years, I started to delve into questions of real and virtual spatial experiences through the transfer of two-dimensional planimetric drawings of interior spaces, real-world and fictional objects, into three-dimensional objects that were mounted either as single objects or as an ensemble of corresponding pieces on walls, evoking in the spectator's eyes different forms of perception.

At first sight some of the early pieces resembled deconstructivist architecture manifested in a spectacular entanglement of distorted forms and interlaced figures.

In contrast, my work focused on shifting perspectives and changing perceptions through change of the viewer's perspective. If the beholder stands at a right angle straight in front of the object an entirely undistorted version of the three-dimensional pictorial representation appears; one step sideways and the object on the wall unveils its three-dimensional character. What has been originally perceived as a flat surface turns out on closer inspection to be a number of multi-height spatial elements comprising the whole.

90
6 x 6,
1989-1991.
Solid fibreboard, mixed media;
Ø 300 cm

Similar to a closed system of grammar I deployed a coherent system of Euclidian geometry that required strict rules in the making. Taking up Wittgenstein's quote, "the meaning of a word is its use in the language" translates in the case of my work into part-whole relationships of interrelated forms that paradigmatically incorporate different forms and contents, allowing for random possibilities of combination and interpretations.

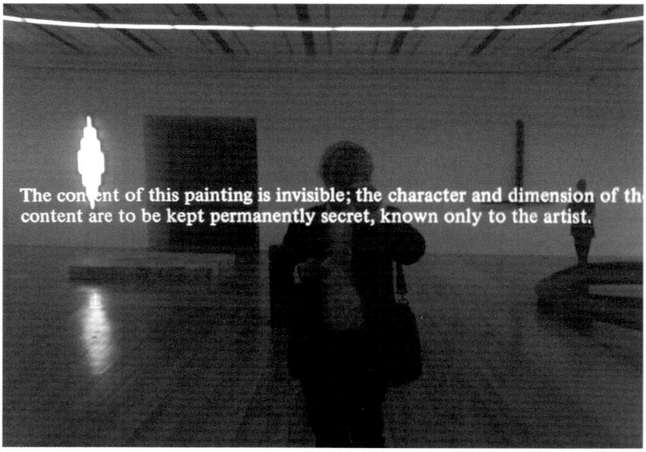

91
Untitled,
2006. Color print, 21 x 15 cm

4

bibliography
list of illustrations

Bibliography

Anderson, C. (2006), The Long Tail: Why the Future of Business is Selling Less of More. New York: Hyperion.

Barabási, A.-L. (2003), Linked: How Everything Is Connect ed to Everything Else and What It Means for Business, Science, and Everyday Life. NY: Plume Books.

Barthes, R. (1970), L'Empire des signes. Skira: Paris.

Baudrillard, J. (2005), The Conspiracy of Art: Manifestos, Interviews. Edited by Sylvere Lotringer and Translated by Ames Hodges. New York: Semiotext(e).

Bauman Z. (1998), Globalization – The Human Consequences. Cambridge: Polity.

Beck, U. (1986), Risikogesellschaft. Auf dem Weg in eine an dere Moderne. Frankfurt a/M: Suhrkamp.

Benkler, Y. (2006), The Wealth of Networks: How Social Production Transforms Markets and Freedom. Yale Press.

Nelson, C., Stamberger, J., Stecker, B. (2011), The Evolution of Hastily Formed Networks for Disaster Response. Conference paper 2011 IEEE Global Humanitarian Technology Conference.

Bolter, D., Grusin, R. (2000), Remediation: Understanding New Media. Cambridge, MA: MIT Press.

Carr, N. (2008), Is Google Making Us Stupid? What the Internet is doing to our brains. The Atlantic.

Chandler, A. (2005), Animating the Social: Mobile Image/Kit Galloway and Sherrie Rabinowitz, p. 153. In: Chandler, A., Neumark, N. (2005), At a Distance. Precursors to Art and Activism on the Internet. Cambridge, Massachusetts: The MIT Press.

Curtis, G. (2007), The Cave Painters: Probing the Mysteries of the World's First Artists. New York: Random House.

Deleuze, G., Guattari, F. (1994), A Thousand Plateaus: Capitalism and Schizophrenia. Minnesota: University of Minnesota Press.

Dewey, J. (1966), Democracy and education: An introduction to the philosophy of education. New York: Free Press.

Düllo, T., Liebl F. (2005), Cultural Hacking. Die Kunst des strategischen Handelns. Vienna, New York: Springer.

Foucault, M. (1978), Discipline & Punish: The Birth of the Prison. New York: Random House.

Frey et al. (2010), Reading and the Brain: What Early Childhood Educators Need to Know. Springer Science+Business Media.

Gershenfeld, N. (2000), When Things Start to Think. New York: Henry Holt.

Gibson, W. (1984), Neuromancer. New York: Penguin.

Groys, B. (2000), Unter Verdacht. Eine Phänomenologie der Medien. München: Carl Hanser Verlag.

Gupta, V. (2009), A Pirate's Platform. blog.leashless.org/65.

Haugeland, J. (1998), Having Thought: Essays in the Metaphysics of Mind, Cambridge, MA: Harvard University Press.

Jenkins, H. (2006), Convergence Culture: Where Old and New Media Collide. New York: New York University Press.

Klein, N. (1999), No Logo: Taking Aim at the Brand Bullies. New York: Pica- dor.
Kittler, F. (1997), Literature, Media, Information Systems (Critical Voices in Art, Theory and Culture). Amsterdam: OPA.

Kurzweil, R. (2005), The Singularity Is Near: When Humans Transcend Biology. New York: Penguin.

Levy, P. (1998), Becoming Virtual: Reality in the Digital Age. New York: Plenum Trade.

Lohmann I. (1998), Strukturwandel der Bildung in der Informationsgesellschaft. www.bildung.com.

Luhmann, N. (1996), Die Realität der Massenmedien. Opladen: Westdeutscher Verlag.

Manovich, L., Kratky, A. (2005) Soft Cinema: Navigating the Database. Cambridge, MA: MIT Press.

Nakashima T., et al. (2009), Book flipping scanning. Conference paper.

Papanek, V. (1971), Design for the Real World: Human Ecology and Social Change. New York: Pantheon Books.

Paper, S. (1993), The Children's Machine. New York: Basic Books.

Sonvilla-Weiss, S. (2008), (IN)VISIBLE. Learning to Act in the Metaverse. Vienna, New York: Springer.

Sonvilla-Weiss, S. (2010), Mashup Cultures. Vienna, New York: Springer.

Stallmann, R. (1985), The GNU Manifesto. www.gnu.org.

Steiner, G. (1996), No Passion Spent: Essays 1978–1996. London: Faber and Faber.

Stephenson, N. (1992), Snow Crash. New York: Bentham.

Ströhl, A. (2002), Vilém Flusser writings. Minneapolis: University of Minnesota Press.

Tapscott, D., Williams, A. (2008), Wikinomics: How Mass Collaboration Changes Everything. New York: Penguin.

Ulatowska, L. (2010), A Rights-Based Global Economy. www.worldcitizens.org.

Virilio, P. (1996), Fluchtgeschwindigkeit. München: Hanser.

Waldrop, M. (1992), Complexity: The Emerging Science at the Edge of Order and Chaos. NY: Touchstone.

Weibel, P. (2004), Gamma und Amplitude: medien- und kunsttheoretische Schriten. Berlin: Fundus.

Wittgenstein L. (1922), Tractatus Logico-Philosophicus. www.gutenberg.org.

Žižek, S. (1989), The Sublime Object of Ideology. London: Verso.

List of illustrations
Source: the author unless otherwise indicated

FRONTISPIECE 1991–2011 (2011). Cover design.
1. The process of meaning (2009). Color print.
2. O and ..., (2003). Sketch from the visual diaries.
3. Untitled (2011). Color print.
4. Search-cube (2011). The Visual Search Engine.
5. Lions, bear, ca. 30,000 B.C. Chauvet cave paintings
6. Out-of-body (2011). Still from the animation.
7. Brain-Computer-Interface (BCI), 2010. Technische Universität Berlin.
8. Cybernetic drawings, 2003. Detail from the sketchbook.
9. Stills from the recorded flip-book exercises (2010).
10. Book flipping scanning system (2010). University of Tokyo.
11. Repair (2007). Sketch book drawing detail.
12. No entrance for human beings (2011). Draft for a wall design.
13. Design of a PGP word list (2010). Color print.
14. Inside-Outside (2011). Infographics.
15. Suspicion (2011). Infographics.
16. Public key (2011). Infographics.
17. CAPTCHA design (2011).
18. Air seats 2012 (2011). Concept design.
19. Social media distributed systems model (2011).
20. Still from the animation Aesthetics of Uncertainty (2010).
21. Screenshot from flickr website (2010).
22. Data mashups, Infographics (2010).
23. Still from Peter Greenaway's short movie Intervals (1969).
24. Soft Cinema, 2003. Installation commissioned and produced by ZKM.
25. Plot structure of the film Memento (2009).
26. Stills from the collaborative movie Life in Day (2010).
27. Technical Difficulties (2010). Concept work.
28. The Internet of Things (2009). Concept work.
29. Quick Response (2010). Mobile design study.
30. Victor Papanek Tin Can Radio (1962).
31. XO laptop (2005). Design sketch
32. Ad hoc networks (2008). Infographics.
33. Material, immaterial value chain (2010). Concept design.
34. Public (2009). Concept design.
35. Change is gonna happen (2007). Public intervention Ghent.
36. Pillow flashmob, Berlin.
37. Open Systems (2010). Infographics
38. Untitled (1995). Photo object.
39. Seoul #12 (2008). Color print.
40. Seoul #18 (2008). Color print.
41. India #5 (2009). Color print.
42. India #6 (2009). Color print.
43. India #7 (2009). Color print.
44. India #18 (2009). Color print.
45. Stefan Sonvilla-Weiss Arbeiten (1997). Interactive CD-Rom.
46. Borromini Interactive (1999). Flash game design.
47. Bach (1994). Animated drawings.

48. Stills from the animation Fruits (1997).
49. Body-Fruits (1997). Drawing, photography.
50. Land (1993). Color print, transparency film.
51. Untitled (1997). Computer-aided large scale imagery.
52. Detail from the photo series Fruits (1993).
53. Stills from the animation Morphing (1997).
54. Healing (1994). Mixed media.
55. Detail of Flying Bodies (1994). Transparency film.
56. Trafik (1998). Exhibition view art gallery Szombathely.
57. Family rituals (1993). Photo objects.
58. Feli (1993). Photo objects.
59. Self-Portrait (1992). Color print.
60. Untitled (1993). Color print.
61. Einfach Sein (1993). Exhibition invitation card.
62. Sketches of the working room (1993). Collage.
63. Detail view of the working room (1993). Mixed media. Photo: Rainer Dempf.
64. Installation view of the working room (1993). Mixed media.
65. Installation view of the dining room (1993). Mixed media.
66. Installation view of the sleeping room (1993). Mixed media.
67. Installation view Children's Playground (1993). Photo: Rainer Dempf.
68. Children's Playground #1 (1993). Mixed media. Photo: Rainer Dempf.
69. Liquid Diaries (1993). Mixed media. Photo: Rainer Dempf.
70. Alphabet (1993). Mixed media. Photo: Rainer Dempf.
71. Children's Playground #2 (1993). Mixed media. Photo: Rainer Dempf.
72. Children's Playground #3 (1993). Mixed media. Photo: Rainer Dempf.
73. Children's Playground #4 (1993). Mixed media. Photo: Rainer Dempf.
74. Children's Playground #5 (1993). Mixed media. Photo: Rainer Dempf.
75. Children's Playground #8 (1993). Detail view. Photo: Rainer Dempf.
76. Studio view Vienna (1994). Color print.
77. Synthetic Kneelers (1991). Mixed media. Contemporary Art Space Vienna.
78. Instructions (1991). Mixed media. Exhibition view. Photo: Rainer Dempf.
79. Installation View (1991). Contemporary Art Space Vienna.
80. Liquid Boxes (1991). Contemporary Art Space Vienna.
81. Installation piece (1991). Studio view Vienna. Photo: Rainer Dempf.
82. New York #7 (1991). Photograph.
83. New York #14 (1991). Photograph
84. New York Diaries (1991-1992). Mixed media. Photo: Rainer Dempf.
85. Studio View, Vienna (1991). Photo: Rainer Dempf.
86. Fractal Innocence (1990-1991). Installation view Haus Wittgenstein.
87. Insight (1991). Installation view with the artist. Haus Wittgenstein.
88. Installation view (1991). Haus Wittgenstein.
89. Open Box #1 (1991). Installation view Haus Wittgenstein.
90. 6 x 6 (1989-1991). Mixed media. Photo: Rainer Dempf.
91. Untitled (2006). Color print.